Finance on a Beermat

Stephen King has built a  up, is a Chartered Accountant ick Business School. His cu de f-works.co.uk, which p to businesses doing something new, exciting or different.

Jeff Macklin has been involved in the start-up of a number of international and UK-based businesses. He is currently Chairman of FDUK and Finance Director of a major UK drainage repair company. He is a Certified Public Accountant and has an MBA from Drexel University, Philadelphia.

Chris West is a professional writer, with a background in marketing and PR. He has written fiction and books on business, personal development, writing good English and travel. He is co-author of the best-selling *The Beermat Entrepreneur* and sole author of *Marketing on a Beermat*.

Praise for *Finance on a Beermat*

'My eyes glaze over at the very mention of financial matters, so I'm extremely happy that Steve, Jeff and Chris have written this book for me and anyone else who gets scared at the very mention of money.' **Dan Germain, co-founder, innocent drinks**

'Every new business owner should read this book.' **Andy Raynor, chief executive, Tenon Group**

'Another must-read from the inspirational team that brought us other *Beermat* classics. As always, easy to digest but stays with you forever.' **Matt Williams, founder and chief executive, Making Waves Communications**

'*Finance on a Beermat* builds a much-needed bridge between finance professionals and working entrepreneurs.' **Tony Gibbens, senior private banker, Coutts & Co**

'At last! Finance truly demystified. Credit to the authors for turning a boring subject full of jargon into something more palatable.' **Gita Patel, director, Stargate Capital**

'... a must for all entrepreneurs, a great source of tips for existing organisations and a ready made set of handbooks for companies that are already true *Beermat* businesses!' **Joe Nicholson, managing director, Anvil Software Ltd**

'The authors' advice in this excellent volume should be essential reading for any new, or even any existing, business.' **Garry Mumford, senior partner, Insight Associates**

'An excellent introduction to what is for many a daunting subject – approachable, concise and relevant.' **Tim Jones, chief excecutive, pada**

'Finance can be a minefield for the entrepreneur. Here is a clear, expertly-drawn map that will lead you safely through it.' **Chris Stevens, managing director, Eteach UK Ltd**

'A book on finance that I could understand and actually enjoyed reading. Hallelujah!' **Andrew Dixon, chief executive of Newcastle Gateshead Initiative**

'Clear, to the point and very readable.' **Kevin Jones, partner, Clarke Willmott**

'The classic *Beermat* formula – simple points, made by experts who have been there and done it, expressed in clear, elegant prose. Another success.' **Simon Bragg, joint chief executive, Oriel Securities Ltd**

Finance on a
Beermat

Stephen King, Jeff Macklin
&
Chris West

BUSINESS
BOOKS

To Jayne, Diane and Rayna

Published by Random House Business Books 2008

4 6 8 10 9 7 5

First published in Great Britain in 2006 by
Random House Business Books

This edition published in Great Britain in 2008 by
Random House Business Books
Random House, 20 Vauxhall Bridge Road,
London SW1V 2SA

www.randomhouse.co.uk

Addresses for companies within The Random House Group Limited can be found at:
www.randomhouse.co.uk/offices.htm

The Random House Group Limited Reg. No. 954009

A CIP catalogue record for this book
is available from the British Library

ISBN 9781847940070

Typeset in Foundry Form Sans and Bembo
Design and make-up by Roger Walker
Printed and bound in the UK by
CPI Group (UK) Ltd, Croydon, CR0 4YY

Contents

(= List of things you will understand by the end of this book)

Author's Note

This book has been more of a team effort than any Beermat book so far. Some authors find larger collaborations heavy going, but this has been hugely enjoyable – and not just because of some excellent team dinners. We all hope it will be as much fun to read as it was to write: quite an aspiration for a book on finance, but we wish it all the same.

We've all had all kinds of support – most of all from our families, but also from various helpful and enthusiastic friends and colleagues. My agent David Grossman and our editors Clare Smith and Tiffany Stansfield have done their usual excellent work, and thanks must go to the following people who kindly read through versions of the manuscript and made comments: Michael Citroen, Richard Clarke, Ian Colquhoun, Clare Heathcote, Mike Jones, James Lott, Ian Rummels, Norman Smith, Tony Taylor and Robert Whittington.

Chris West, Cambridge 2006

Introduction: **Fear of Finance**

Entrepreneurs and small business proprietors are brave people. You have to be brave to turn your back on the relative safety of regular employment and go it alone (or, if you want to succeed, go it as part of a small, dedicated team). You have to be brave to deal with the hassles, with the bureaucracy, with the Monday mornings when you open the order book and see blank pages two weeks ahead. Forget those 'charismatic CEOs' we're always hearing about in the media: the real heroes and heroines of contemporary economic life are entrepreneurs and small-business leaders.

But even they have their weak spots, where their daily-proven courage suddenly melts. Spiders? Heights? Lifts? No doubt, for some. But more common, and much more terrifying, than any of these is...

Finance.

Entrepreneurs love *doing* things. They have an idea; they follow it through. If the idea has 'the magic', it starts to take off: orders flow in, there are queues round the block, overloaded servers crash, etc. This is the ultimate buzz for the entrepreneur, who'll be revelling in the moment, but also thinking ahead to how he or she can do it even better in the future, how different markets could be served in a similar way, how...

What the entrepreneur won't be thinking about is finance: the paperwork, invoices, receipts, all that dull stuff.

Except, of course, that stuff is worse than dull. It's threatening. The paperwork is the only thing that will tell them whether the idea is sustainable. Is all this busy-ness actually making money? Can it be built into a real, thriving business? (Busy-ness to business – the great transition…) Or will it all go pop, like so many brilliant ideas?

Finance people have the answers to those questions. But they're scary, too. 'I dread going to my accountant,' admits one entrepreneur. 'It's like being sent for by the headmaster. Even if you're not sure what you've done, you know it's going to be bad news.'

Accountants connive in the naughty schoolkid/headmaster role play. They often dress very formally, and almost always speak jargon. 'You should be capitalising more intangibles straight to the balance sheet' – that's 100 lines for a start, and possibly detention, and you still haven't a clue what they're on about.

Worse, like the best headmasters, accountants know stuff that by rights they shouldn't. They can look at your accounts and tell you all sorts of things about your business that you didn't know (or, more frightening still, that you did know but didn't think anyone else could find out).

And they're inescapable. The day you leave school you can turn your back on headmasters: many entrepreneurs do that, being doers not academics. But you can't turn your back on accountants. The taxman and the VAT man are waiting. They need to hear from you; if they don't, they're going to come looking – in packs, howling… There's the bank, too. You might persuade your bank to lend you money on a good rapport, an even better idea and a nicely-crafted business plan. But soon the bank manager is going to want to see real figures. Accounts.

Finance is nemesis. It's fate, lying in wait for those who choose to ignore it. A world of headmasters with dark, magical powers whom you can't ignore. No wonder so many people are terrified of it.

Of course, they shouldn't be, and the purpose of this book is to lay that fear to rest. Good finance is at the heart of a successful business. So don't fear it, embrace it. We'll show you how, and even how to make the embrace heartfelt.

The Beermat context

This book is based on a model of business development outlined in Mike and Chris's first book, *The Beermat Entrepreneur.* You don't have to agree with every point of this model to find this book useful, but an understanding of 'where we're coming from' will help. If you are not familiar with the model, here is a brief outline.

The classic Beermat enterprise starts with an entrepreneur and one or two friends, after a discussion in a pub. For the venture to succeed, the entrepreneur needs to expand this to a *balanced business team*, specialising in the core areas of business:

Sales

Finance

Technical – operations (also referred to as 'delivery')

▶▶

Technical – innovation (if in IP/technology-based business) or some other specific factor critical to the success of the business.

The members of this team are the *cornerstones* of the business (one of them will probably be the *foil* to the entrepreneur, a clear 'number two' in the organisation). They are all experts at the specialisms, and must be given stakes and influence in the business.

However, the first thing to do is not to complete the team – this can be done over time – but to complete the 'Original Beermat': the three things you must define about your business to get it going. First is your *elevator pitch* – a brief summary of exactly what it is you do, for whom, and why should they buy it from you. A good starting point is to ask the *entrepreneur's magic question*: 'Where's the pain?' Where are customers incurring cost, waste and aggravation? Where are they missing opportunities, getting lousy service, having to search hard for information, losing their own customers, furious because they can't find a particular item (and so on)?

The second item on the Original Beermat is the *mentor* for your business, a senior and respected business person whom you like, who likes you, and who will give you advice and open doors for you.

Third, you need a *first customer*. Clearly this will be notional on the first evening you come up ▶▶

with the business idea, but the point is to get a real customer as soon as possible. Next morning, if you can. This holds true for all kinds of start-up, even manufacturing. No sales, no revenue, no business.

Once you have a first, paying customer, you work with them to write a *White Paper*. What was it like for the customer? How did they actually use your product? (By 'product', we don't just mean a thing, but your *total provision of a customer benefit*, probably via a mixture of things and services.) What did they find particularly helpful? What did they dislike or end up not using? How could what you do be improved? This will help you refine the product itself, the elevator pitch and your understanding of the real market you are in.

Up to the point where a business comprises its entrepreneur and four cornerstones, plus maybe an office manager/receptionist, it is in its *seedling* phase. After that, it grows to about 25 people, retaining its entrepreneurial 'feel' in what we call the *sapling* phase. At this point, the business then has to decide if it wants to stay small and friendly – a 'boutique', often a pleasant and highly profitable way to do business – or to get its head down and go for growth. The cultural consequences of choosing the latter option are massive.

If it makes the leap, it becomes (to keep the metaphor going) a tree. Up to about 150 people, ▶▶

it is a *young tree*. During this phase, full-blown systems have to be set up, and the entrepreneur and cornerstones have to consider their own roles: they may now be burnt out and/or getting in the way. Beyond 150 people, we have a *mighty oak*, and have moved beyond the scope of the Beermat model – except that the business is now big enough for the whole creative process to start again, via internal entrepreneurs (intrapreneurs).

The Beermat Entrepreneur put forward clear, and controversial, views about funding. Beermat businesses fund from revenue. If they are in a capital-intensive area, they may not be able to achieve this, but should strive to do so by all means possible.

Finally, the book expressed a philosophy of business. It's about creating long-term value for yourself, your people and your customers: 'win-win situations', to use the jargon. Beermat enterprises are ethical, fair, fun to work in – and make lots of money.

Beermat.biz

Chapter One: A Finance Cornerstone

The first thing you, as an entrepreneur, can do to banish your fear of finance is to commit to finding a real *finance cornerstone* for your business.

What do we mean by this?

A cornerstone is an expert on an aspect of business who has real leadership input into the venture. He or she is not just an outsider who gets wheeled in at odd (and often inappropriate) moments, but a team member with whom the key issues of both long-term strategy and daily tactics are thrashed out. The sales, finance, operations and innovation/critical factor cornerstones are people who live the business almost as much as their leader, the entrepreneur. In an ideal Beermat company, they each own 20 per cent of the business. Yes, real companies often fall short of this ideal, but, if the cornerstone does have a smaller stake, his or her input should be taken as seriously as if he or she owned 20 per cent: their knowledge is worth that much.

The Beermat business begins with three friends sitting in a pub discussing business ideas – again, perhaps an ideal, but the point is that if an entrepreneur has an idea, he or she must get a team of able, liked and trusted people around them as soon as possible. One of these early people must understand finance.

What does the finance cornerstone bring to the party?

A lot more than a neat set of *books and annual accounts*, though finance people can do these standing on their head, of course.

Management information. Finance cornerstones soon become the expert at 'what is really going on in the business'. They then tell everyone else, through formal means like monthly management accounts, and informally via conversations, emails etc.

Cash control. Running out of cash is the biggest single cause of small business failure. But most entrepreneurs lack the specialist skills – or the time – to manage cash, the lifeblood of the growing business.

Cost control. Every business owner/manager knows that sinking feeling of looking at an invoice and wondering how the hell they ended up being charged that amount for something. Finance people can prevent this.

Administration. In many start-ups or small businesses, essential tasks such as HR (human resources) or IT management get ignored or done half-heartedly. The team are all busy: they have more important things to do, like making or selling things; that other admin stuff can wait. But wait too long, and the infrastructure of the business begins to collapse. Finance people get this done, well and without fuss.

Tax. They'll also deal with stuff entrepreneurs hate, like VAT and PAYE.

Law. Finance people usually know more about this than anyone else on the team and, even more important, know someone who's a real expert.

Decision support. Entrepreneurs are always coming up with ideas. This is as it should be, but these ideas need to be assessed objectively. Finance people have the skills and mindset to do this.

Strategic input. Finance cornerstones help the entrepreneur craft a business model and develop that model as the market and the business change. Yes, some entrepreneurs do this themselves, and pride themselves on it. But many don't. Many great, public-figure entrepreneurs rely on a skilled finance person who shuns the limelight while turning busy-ness into business. McDonalds, for example, is often cited as a great one-man entrepreneurial achievement, but actually was going nowhere until the famous figurehead entrepreneur Ray Kroc teamed up with Harry Sonneborn, a finance cornerstone. Kroc was a great ops man, who perfected the delivery model with precise times for flipping burgers, recipes for sauces and so on. Sonneborn turned it into a business.

Funding. Finance people know how to *raise money*. They know when to raise money, where to raise money, and what sort of money to raise. They manage the often tricky relationship between start-up and bank (and any other capital providers/grant givers).

Finance cornerstone roles on a Beermat

★ Bookkeeping and annual accounts

★ Management information

★ Cash control　▶▶

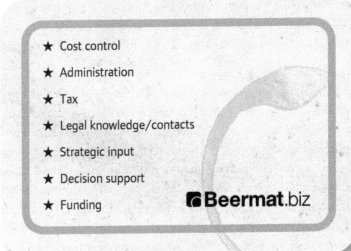

★ Cost control

★ Administration

★ Tax

★ Legal knowledge/contacts

★ Strategic input

★ Decision support

★ Funding

Beermat.biz

What sort of people are finance cornerstones?

Most are qualified chartered, certified or 'cost and management' accountants: ACA, ACCA, ACMA respectively, or fellows of these associations (FCA, FCCA, FCMA) if they are older. However, these qualifications on their own do not guarantee a person is right for the job: other things are needed.

They must have the right *experience*. This should be varied, with sufficient knowledge of big companies to see where a growing business is headed, but with their main emphasis on start-ups or small/medium-sized enterprises (SMEs). Some such people never had the time or inclination to finish their exams, and will be part-qualified.

Experience *in your sector* is nice to have but not essential. Entrepreneurs often insist on this, but they are wrong to – unless nobody else in the team has sector experience (in which case they will need a mentor who is also an insider).

They *like working in SMEs*. People hankering for a return to a big corporate or an accountancy practice, and just looking for work with a small/medium-sized company until the opportunity for such a return comes along, will not be right.

The differences between life in the finance department of a big company, and life as the finance cornerstone of a start-up or SME are considerable. In the large corporation:

★ You're part of a large, hierarchical team

★ You use only existing, complex systems and processes

★ Cash management is a part of the job, but often overridden by powerful lobbies of technologists or by marketing people eager to build brands through expensive advertising

★ Only the top people have any input into strategy

While in the start-up or SME:

★ You start on your own (with an assistant later as the business grows)

★ Systems will be initially cheap and simple – but you can design your own

★ Cash management is your most important job (and you have to be ruthless)

★ You have huge input into strategy

The best finance cornerstones understand and *enjoy strategy*, taking an overview of business issues. If the entrepreneur is not a strategist, this is essential. If the entrepreneur is a strategist, it is still good for them to have someone else in the team who understands the subject.

Finance cornerstones should have the right *personality*. They need to be *relaxed* enough to take off their tie and roll up their sleeves – many entrepreneurs threw away their ties years ago. But at the same time they must *take more responsibility* than most accountants. They have to have enough sense of *adventure* to share the buzz of the entrepreneur and his or her team: they will have decided that life's too short just to plod along ruts worn by other people. They must also accept that doing things differently will involve increased risk (their job is all about minimising risk, of course, but they know it's always there and live with it). They are *not after power*, but enjoy getting stuff done. They are happy dealing with *details*. They also need to be *big* enough to take occasional bouts of entrepreneurial petulance.

Of course, they will have, and be proud of, complete *integrity*.

And, of course, you, the entrepreneur, and your finance cornerstone have to *like one another*. This doesn't follow in a corporate, where senior people can develop hatreds that make Gordon Brown and Tony Blair look like bosom pals but the place still functions. In the start-up, personal animosity at the top is a recipe for disaster.

So to sum up, what you need is someone with whom you can build a long-term relationship based on respect, on a shared enjoyment of the journey of building a business, on complete trust, and on a bit of personal chemistry.

Part-time cornerstones

From the box opposite, finding such a person might seem a tall order, let alone persuading them to come and work for your start-up. You don't know anyone like that. Or maybe you do, and they're earning £80,000 a year. You can't even dream of paying someone that.

So don't. Get a *part-time* finance cornerstone: someone with the above skills and character, but who looks after you and a number

Finance cornerstones on a Beermat

Must have:

★ Professional skill

★ The right experience (specific sector experience nice but not essential)

★ Liking for SMEs

★ Strategic understanding

Personality:

★ Relaxed

★ Prepared to do detailed stuff

★ Responsible

★ Adventurous

★ Accept risk

★ Don't crave power

★ Like getting things done

★ 'Big'

★ Trustworthy

And you must like them!

Beermat.biz

of other businesses. There are an increasing number of such people around. As you grow, he or she may have to choose whether to join you full-time or to hand over to another finance expert. But that's a long way in the future. Right now, look around for someone of the right calibre, who will start by coming in one day a month.

The 'day' would probably involve a half-day looking at books and talking to the team, plus the odd chat during the month. The spirit of this deal must be gentlemanly, the opposite to one where a clock is ticking: the cornerstone usually ends up putting in more than eight hours, but if he or she feels they are being over-used, they know they can go back to the entrepreneur and have a discussion, the result of which should be more money – say two days' worth. (Or fewer phone calls? Best not: if the cornerstone's advice is really proving that valuable, pay for it.)

This may now sound like too little input, but it's amazing what value the right person can add in this time.

Where do you look?

Accountants tend to work in two environments: *commercial*, where they are part of the management team of a business, or *professional*, which means they work in accountancy firms carrying out audits or providing highly specialist advice on topics such as tax. The commercial accountant aspires to be FD, or even CEO, of their employer; the professional accountant aspires to be a partner in his or her practice. (Note the potential confusion here. People not acquainted with the jargon naturally assume that the term 'professional' covers everyone whose profession is accountancy, whether the person works for a chain of garages or Deloittes. This is wrong. When finance people use the term, they only mean a subset of accountants, the ones who work in accountancy practices.)

By and large, the profession is not the place to look for finance cornerstones. The mindset is not commercial enough. Specialists (e.g. on tax) are too specialised: brain surgeons are not GPs. Auditors are too conservative – not surprising, as they are there to make sure the rest of us adhere to the rules. An auditor's approach to something you can't do tends to be to shake his or her head and say, 'Sorry, you can't do that; look, it says here in Rule 46B…' The commercial accountant is on the lookout for a smart, and still legal, way round the problem.

Big recruitment agencies aren't the right source, either. These organisations are fine if you are a large company seeking someone full-time but temporary, to manage a project or fill a gap while a regular FD is unavailable for six months. Start-ups and SMEs have different needs.

Now, smaller businesses are emerging that have understood the finance leadership needs of the start-up/SME sector, and specialise in matching small, ambitious businesses with able part-time FDs. We declare an interest here: Jeff and Steve run one such company, FDUK (www.fduk.co.uk), based in Bristol but now operating nationally. But they are not alone. Other players in this field include:

★ Secantor (www.secantor.com), focused on the Midlands

★ F-Works (www.f-works.co.uk), based in Bristol

★ FDYL (www.financedirectors.co.uk), based in Yorkshire

★ Insight Associates (www.insightassociates.co.uk), based in Essex

Another option is to go out and find a finance cornerstone yourself. If you have good networking skills – and as an entrepreneur you will either need to have such skills or to ally yourself very closely to someone with these skills – then you've got what it takes to find the right person.

Start in your personal network. Do you know anyone who's an accountant? Go and talk to them. They may not be cornerstone material, but they may know someone who is.

If this yields nothing, join a local networking group. There are loads of these, from the traditional Chambers of Commerce to online networks. The latter in particular tend to be full of 'consultants', skilled people looking for opportunities to exercise that skill. Some will be commercial accountants, looking for part-time finance cornerstone roles.

The right person will fit the bill above, both in terms of skill and of character. You will get on; they will understand your business idea, be genuinely excited about it and eager to be involved.

The deal

Even a day of the right person's time is expensive: £500 a day or more. (This is more than their day-rate when full-time, but they will want extra because the part-timer's life is less certain.) Don't be scared off by this. Remember that one day is all you want per month to start with. And offer a package instead of pure cash:

★ Buzz – the right sort of person will find making a difference in a start-up fun

★ The prospect of serious equity

★ Some money for the moment

A seedling entrepreneur or, better, a seedling entrepreneur with a team of, say, a sales person and an operations expert, could try the following approach: 'We really like you and you seem to like us. We want you to be a proper finance cornerstone, part of the team, from now on, with a serious stake in the company as soon as we know we're a real team. For now, can you spare us a day a month? And supposing we pay you £250 a month for starters, and look at things again in six months?'

Note that in London you might have to offer a slightly larger figure, but, even there, the right person should find this attractive.

Discuss expectations early, and agree on:

★ The immediate deal – how much time for how much money

★ The full deal – if things go well, how much equity will be granted, and when

★ Areas of responsibility. See the list on page 8: the cornerstone should help with all of these

★ When things will be reviewed

★ What will happen if things don't work out

Though you should only be having this discussion with someone you like and trust, ask them for a couple of references from other small businesses they have helped (or are helping). This is standard practice: they won't be offended.

We suggest an initial period of six months, after which you should decide if the person is really right for you long-term (and they can decide if you are right for them long-term). If you both agree that this is the case – and in our experience it usually is – offer the cornerstone equity and start paying them more. If the answer from *either* side is 'no', then agree to shake hands and go your separate ways. This can and should be amicable.

Note that if the business really takes off, you may need to accelerate this process and make the decision earlier than six months: you need your cornerstones solidly in place as you are in for an exciting, but possibly bumpy, ride. Don't be afraid to do this. And congratulations – it sounds like you've got a winner!

Sapling or young tree business entrepreneurs who have got by without a finance cornerstone up to now, but who read this and decide to find one, are a) lucky to have got so far without one and b) in a better position to pay the new cornerstone more. The company will probably need the cornerstone more, too – a couple of days a month, or more for flourishing, young tree businesses. At the same time, the shareholders will be less happy to offer large equity stakes. The cornerstone will understand this, but should still be offered a stake and a board position once the entrepreneur and the rest of the team are satisfied the appointment is right. The head of finance is too important to be a simple hired hand.

At the other end of the scale, less ambitious entrepreneurs, people who are good at doing something and simply want to make a living out of that as sole traders won't need to fork out this amount for financial help, and aren't in a position to offer equity either. But they still need financial input. Can you persuade someone of the above calibre to be your business mentor? Or seek out a less ambitious cornerstone: a bright bookkeeper will have insight into these issues. The need for access to someone who has financial knowledge and with whom you can regularly discuss financial issues exists for all business founders, however grand or humble their plans.

Advice for cornerstones

If you are a potential finance cornerstone looking for the mix we mentioned – of fun, potential upside and some money for the moment – follow the same route as an entrepreneur. Check out the part-time FD companies (or any others that you know). At the same time, start looking in your personal network. There may be entrepreneurs in there; maybe they've read this book and are desperate for exactly what you offer!

Don't be put off looking in your network because it is considered to be 'cheating', because 'real professionals go out there into the marketplace and stand or fall by their skills'. It is both easier and nicer to work among people you know, like and trust.

If you draw a blank in your immediate network, talk to friends, to see if they know anyone they can recommend who is looking for a finance cornerstone. If 'one degree of separation' fails, then get on the general networking trail. (If you're not an experienced networker, start by coming along to one of the Beermat Monday networking sessions we operate in major cities. Details on www.beermat.biz) Don't forget to use and value your intuition. If you meet an entrepreneur with a great-sounding idea but there's something about them that gives you the creeps, walk away. Your valuable skills will be better used elsewhere. If you're not sure whether you like them, give yourself a little time to work them out, perhaps by offering to do a day's consultancy for them.

An analogy has been made with dating. You are looking to make a serious and life-changing commitment. So take your time, trust your instincts, get out if you realise you've made a horrible mistake. Don't promise too much too soon: if things feel right, let your mutual commitment build. Luckily, start-ups don't require quite the same level of fidelity as sexual partners – but if the start-up is a winner, it will end up taking all your work time, so the analogy isn't that inaccurate.

Early on, 'play the field', working with a few companies as their virtual finance cornerstone. Build a portfolio of clients. You won't be able to serve more than five customers properly – four is enough for most people. So you must ensure that you have a balanced portfolio of start-ups who will only want that one day a month, and of larger businesses, who will want (and pay you for) more work (a growing young tree will want you at least a day a week). Remember to allow yourself at least a day per working week not working for anyone, but keeping your own admin, contacts and knowledge up to date.

You might want to vary your remuneration across your portfolio, depending on your attitude to risk and your financial commitments. Have some jobs that you do for cash, and others where you take less cash (still ask for some!) but receive an equity stake.

If you have several stakes, and one of the businesses begins to take off so much that you need to work for them full-time, you may need to sell your other stakes. Make sure this is understood from the start by all concerned (and that each shareholders' agreement has a clear, agreed procedure in place to do this).

A different route

If all the above material seems obvious, consider what so many businesses do. They start off without a finance person in sight. After a while, they 'get someone in to do the books'. This person does a competent and professional job gathering up the scribbled invoices and orders and making them into a proper set of books. They balance these books. They may even do a spot of credit control, chasing up some debtors. They are offered, and therefore provide, as much strategic input into the business as the office cleaner (assuming the office has a cleaner, which in many cases it doesn't, as nobody has got round to organising one).

If things go wrong, these passive bookkeepers simply say, 'I did what you asked me to do: I balanced the books'. They may not have spotted the trouble brewing; or if they did spot it, they kept quiet, having had the experience of being fired by previous employers whom they tried to warn off from suicidal courses of action.

Businesses going down this road will also take on a firm of accountants when an emergency crops up, such as:

★ They need a Company Secretary

★ They need someone to do their payroll

★ They are worried about VAT

★ They need 'some numbers' for their business plan

★ They need to file accounts with Companies House and/or the Inland Revenue

★ Their bank suddenly asks to see some numbers

★ The entrepreneur suddenly realises the books are a mess

★ 'Everybody else seems to have an accountancy firm, so we'd better get one too'

★ They need a formal audit

After the emergency, they won't see the accountants again until it's time to draw up the next lot of annual accounts.

Of the above list, there is only one item for which professional involvement is essential: audit. Audit is what the profession is for, and best at. But note that the threshold at which the law requires a formal audit has recently been raised from £1m annual turnover to £5.6m.

Companies who think they are going to race to some kind of sale or public offering should be audited from the very start: buyers and investors will want to see three years' audited accounts. Even on the comparatively wild-west Alternative Investment Market (AIM), which doesn't formally require these, you won't get much of a rating without them.

The rest of us – the overwhelming majority of businesses – should wait till they hit that £5.6m mark before they have an audit. It's an expense. A sensible estimate is £1,000 per £1m turnover, with a minimum of £2,000. If you are running the business properly, audit will not yield any useful information:

effectively you are being charged to be investigated for incompetence (deliberate or otherwise).

One objection might be that lenders like to see audited accounts – this is true, for companies without a finance cornerstone. Lenders are rightly afraid of organisations where nobody has in-depth financial knowledge. Our experience is that once there's a finance expert on board, nobody's worried about audit.

The finance cornerstone can deal with *all* the other issues above, so should deal with them. He or she is a core part of your team, batting for you. 'Profession' accountants are hired hands (safe hands, but not your hands...). You will see your finance cornerstone every month, and probably talk to him or her every week, whereas many entrepreneurs – no doubt driven by fear of finance – only see their accountancy firm once a year, a fact we find truly shocking.

The business with no finance cornerstone will have other woes, too. Audited accounts or no, it will have a rocky relationship with its bank manager. The entrepreneur will despise the manager for failing to ignite with the passion for the idea the way he/she and the team have. This relationship will get even worse the first time the company suddenly turns to the bank and asks for more money – from the bank manager's perspective, out of the blue. There will be no real understanding in the business of how money should be spent, about what constitutes a wise decision and what constitutes a foolish one – apart, of course, from after-the-event analysis over a beer with the team. Nor will the team have a clear idea of the financial position of the company. The company will probably hit a series of cash crises, one of which may destroy it, as the bank or a big creditor finally loses patience.

A finance cornerstone, at the heart of the business but initially part-time, should prevent all that.

Of course, we've heard of companies taking on part-time finance cornerstones and the relationship not working. The usual cause of failure is that expectations are not set correctly at the start of the relationship. Sometimes, people just don't get on. Whatever the cause of the breakdown, it is not a reason for abandoning the part-time cornerstone approach, but for doing it better in the future. As an entrepreneur you perpetually have to make judgements and back them. Sometimes these go wrong. Learn the lesson and get it right next time.

We believe strongly that the right finance cornerstone is an enormous asset to any and every business. This book will show entrepreneurs what to expect from this asset (and how to understand what it does), and will also show accountants how to spread their entrepreneurial wings via a cornerstone role.

Accountants and entrepreneurs: oil and water?

Some accountants are put off entering start-ups/ SMEs by the wayward nature of many entrepreneurs. 'I know that entrepreneurs have to be like that to get ideas off the ground,' they say, 'But it's all a bit wild for me.' Such a reaction is fine – they should stay in a large organisation. But if they add, 'Shame, 'cause I'd really like to be involved in something small…' then they are cornerstone material, despite their concerns about entrepreneurs' characters.

▶▶

Business is too complicated a thing for one person to master on their own. There has to be the drive, passion and opportunism of the entrepreneur; there has to be the measure and solidity of the good finance cornerstone. There also has to be the clannishness of the sales person and the workbench meticulousness of an operations cornerstone. Any good business is a collection of people with very different temperaments. (One of the entrepreneur's greatest achievements lies in rallying them all under the one banner of the business.)

Many finance cornerstones end up with a special role – as *foils* to entrepreneurs, their main confidantes and helpers, providing the essential grounding to their more mercurial side. Remember Harry Sonneborn and McDonalds: behind many great entrepreneurs there is a great foil, and he or she is very often a finance cornerstone.

Or maybe they'll just be part of a top team of varied and able people. They should join the team, knowing they are going to be surrounded by different characters, and enjoy the variety!

Very few accountants who have taken the plunge and become finance cornerstones turn round later and regret it.

Beermat.biz

Chapter Two: Accounting 101: the very basics

In this chapter, we look at the basic principles and techniques of accounting. Basic, because that's where fear of finance begins. 'You're an entrepreneur,' people say, 'so you must be able to read a balance sheet.'

Great if you can, but we know many excellent entrepreneurs who can't. Don't be ashamed to be among them – but read on, and change that.

In the process we will make some simplifications: accountants who read this chapter must forgive us for this (or leap straight ahead to Chapter Three).

Double entry

This is the basis of bookkeeping, and thus the correct place to start. It is also the point at which non-accountants begin to feel that first frisson of fear.

Everyone is familiar with the simplest forms of account, the single-entry books kept by tiny organisations. Every transaction is recorded *once*, either as an expenditure (cash out) or as income (cash in). So the Clapham South Literary Appreciation Society spends £25 on local experimental poet Sebastian Dashwood to come and read to them, £75 for the hire of St Bede's Hall, £30 on refreshments, £20 on the bottle of malt whisky Mr Dashwood insists be provided at all his readings. All expenditure. Luckily they take £20 at the door, and receive subscriptions of £50 and a £50 grant from the local arts group. The net result is a shortfall of £30 – which the poetry-loving treasurer makes up from her own pocket.

The whole story is told in eight entries, and the book only balances at the end thanks to the treasurer.

The next stage up from this is the statement we get from our bank. This operates the single-entry system, but adds a column along the right showing the amount in the account at any time. Many small businesses begin with their bank statement as their source of financial information: at the start, this is quite sensible, especially if they are funded by an overdraft. We offer a better, but not dissimilar, suggestion for brand-new businesses in Chapter Three.

Note that this extra column tells you your cash position. For accountants, 'cash' doesn't just mean notes and coins, but also money in bank accounts. From now on, it must mean the same to you, and to everyone else in the business.

Even with the extra cash column, the single-entry system is a very blunt instrument, which will soon be inadequate to the task of presenting a picture of the complex thing that is a growing business. Single entry does not reflect either the supplier invoices you haven't paid yet or the people who owe you money. Single entry makes no distinction between money spent on things that will last for ages, like a 99-year lease on a property, and money that gets used by the business day-to-day, like a box of paperclips. Without these distinctions you will have no idea if you are trading profitably or pouring time and money into a hole (i.e. if this is busy-ness or business).

The unsuitability of single-entry accounts was realised a long time ago, by a monk. This may seem odd, but in the fifteenth century, monasteries were big businesses. A few big brands – Franciscan, Cistercian, Augustinian – slugged it out the way modern multinationals do now. The monk in question was Fra Luca Bartolomeo de Pacioli, and his book, published in 1494, was called *Summa de arithmetica, geometria, proportioni et proportionalita*. In it he outlined (among many things) the basic principles of modern bookkeeping.

Double entry means exactly what it says – that every accounted transaction creates *two* entries in the accounts. These entries are equal, and always ensure that the company retains a balance between its assets and its liabilities, or what it *owns* and what it *owes*.

Let's consider the start of a venture. The first transaction is likely to be you injecting some money into the business to fund future expenditure. The business now owns cash (not just notes and coins, remember, but banked money), which is an *asset*. At the same time, it now owes you, the owner, the money you have put into it, i.e. it has an equal *liability* to repay you at some time in the future. In the double-entry system, both are noted.

Assets (owned)		**Liabilities** (owed)	
Cash	£1000	Share capital	£1000

Let's assume the business uses some of the cash to buy equipment. Again, two entries; one as the cash asset reduces in value, the other as it is replaced by another asset of equal value – equipment. Note that the two entries don't have to be one in each box, as they were above: here they are both in the assets box.

Assets		Liabilities	
Equipment	£ 500		
Cash	£ 500		
Total	£1000	Share capital	£1000

A supplier is approached who offers normal trade terms for some raw materials, and the business takes delivery. Here the two entries are stock – an asset acquired – and a new liability to pay the supplier (who has become a creditor of the business).

Assets		Liabilities	
Equipment	£ 500	Creditor	£ 250
Stock	£ 250		
Cash	£ 500	Share capital	£1000
Total	£1250	Total	£1250

Note: the term creditors is sometimes replaced with 'Accounts Payable', arguably a more graphic term. We will stick with creditors, but feel free to use the alternative if it avoids confusion and makes the reality of creditors – you owe them money! – more alive to you.

When it is necessary, the business will pay the creditor. The creditor entry will thus disappear, and cash will fall to £250.

Assets		Liabilities	
Equipment	£ 500		
Stock	£ 250		
Cash	£ 250	Share capital	£1000
Total	£1000	Total	£1000

£100 worth of the raw material is then made into a product (to keep the example simple, the ops cornerstone does the work and makes no charge to the company). There is no change in the accounts here (though technically the 'stock' category can be subdivided into 'raw materials', 'work in progress' and 'finished goods', and the £100 worth of stuff has progressed from the start to the finish of this three-link chain).

However, if we then sell the product to someone for £150, to be paid in 30 days, we need two more entries. First, we now have a debtor, someone who owes us money (also known as 'Accounts Receivable'). Second, the company has now made its first profit – time to celebrate, though not to get too carried away, as the profit is only on paper at the moment. Put the profit in the liabilities box (it is ultimately owed to the owners, remember).

Assets		Liabilities	
Equipment	£ 500		
Stock	£ 150		
Debtors	£ 150	Share capital	£1000
Cash	£ 250	Profit	£ 50
Total	£1050	Total	£1050

When the debtor pays, *then* it's time to crack open the champagne. This difference, between theoretical profit and actual cash in the bank, will feature over and over again in our discussions about good financial management.

Assets		Liabilities	
Equipment	£ 500		
Stock	£ 150	Share capital	£1000
Cash	£ 400	Profit	£ 50
Total	£1050	Total	£1050

The entrepreneur goes and visits the client, to explain how to use the product more effectively. He/she charges £100 for this piece of consultancy, and is paid on the day with a cheque made out to the business. Pure profit! (And a nice example of why services are such a good business…). Two amended entries: £100 extra cash and £100 extra profit.

Assets		Liabilities	
Equipment	£ 500		
Stock	£ 150	Share capital	£1000
Cash	£ 500	Profit	£ 150
Total	£1150	Total	£1150

And so on. We could go on like this forever, but we hope these two points are now crystal clear:

★ Every single transaction creates two accounting entries…

★ …at the end of which, the assets (owned) and the liabilities (owed) always balance.

If they are not clear, go through the example again (and again, until they are).

The balance sheet

Readers familiar with accounts will recognise the boxes above as an embryonic balance sheet. That is because that's exactly what they are. A balance sheet − even of the biggest corporate behemoth − is the natural and inevitable product of thousands and thousands of balanced double entries, just as a huge coral reef is the natural and inevitable product of thousands and thousands of tiny creatures that have lived there.

So what does this 'coral reef' do? As you'd expect from the above, it answers questions about owning and owing. 'If all our creditors decided to, and were allowed to, walk in tomorrow and take away what they are owed, what would be left for the shareholders?' It answers questions about the company's resilience to changes in fortune, and thus how risky an investment it is.

As with the boxes above, the basics of the balance sheet are assets and liabilities.

Assets

What does the company own? Office fixtures and fittings. Property, machinery and vehicles bought rather than just hired or leased (though if they've been acquired on certain types of lease, they count as 'owned' and must feature in the balance sheet). These are called *fixed assets*.

The company also owns the different types of stock (raw materials, work in progress and finished goods), plus stocks of office stationery, paperclips etc. It owns money owing to it (unless that money is never actually going to be repaid) and cash in the bank. These are all called *current assets*, as it is assumed they won't be in existence in a year's time – even though the stock level may be the same at the end of next year, one must hope it consists of different items.

All the above are called *tangible assets*. There are also *intangible assets*. The list above is fine, but surely one of the greatest assets of a business is the skill of its staff? And what about the loyalty of its customers? The value of its brand name? The answer is that of course these are assets: they're much more important than that rusty old lathe that nobody uses any longer but which is still listed in the balance sheet. But valuing them for balance sheet purposes is almost impossible, so accountants, who value prudence very highly, leave them out. The only time you can put intangible assets in your balance sheet is if you have bought them via a takeover. If you pay £500,000 for a company which owns £200,000 in 'net assets' (see the model balance sheet below for an explanation of this term), you must put the other £300,000 in the balance sheet as what accountants rather quaintly call 'goodwill'.

As a result of this, a balance sheet is a very rough guide to the actual value of a business: companies who grow by acquisition will soon have balance sheets full of goodwill, while a company of equal size that has grown organically will appear smaller. We'll talk more about valuing companies later on.

Note that Enron Corporation, famous for its 'creative' accounting and subsequent collapse, claimed anything and everything as an asset, including planned flows of income from new projects that were then losing money. The company also secured finance via loans from associated companies: thanks to a technicality, such liabilities didn't appear on its balance sheet. As a result the balance sheet made it look like a giant company which owned a lot and owed little, while in fact it was a) smaller and b) much deeper in debt.

Assets are listed in the balance sheet in descending order of permanence. Land comes first, then buildings, then machinery, then motor vehicles ('permanent' provided the sales cornerstone doesn't shunt his new Audi on the M25), then office fixtures and fittings. All will be listed at 'book value', which is their original cost less depreciation (more on this key concept later), except for the land, which will be listed at whatever it was considered to be worth last time it was formally valued.

Among the current assets the hierarchy is: stocks, debtors (a nice assumption that they will soon pay up) and finally cash.

Liabilities

These are what the company owes. As with assets, the key distinction is between short term (any payment that has to be made within one year – money owed to suppliers, the Inland Revenue, a soon-to-expire bank loan) and long term (any payments due later: most large loans should fit this category). A third category of liabilities is what is owed to the shareholders: *shareholders' funds*.

Overleaf is a model balance sheet, simplified in some places, explained in others. Readers with a strong fear-of-finance factor may well grimace on turning the page – but stick with us. It all makes sense, we promise…

The company owns £330,000 worth of fixed assets and £455,000 worth of current assets. It is due to pay out £205,000 to creditors/lenders in the next 12 months, has £150,000 in long-term loans, and the amount left for the shareholders is £430,000.

This balance sheet is recognisable as an evolutionary descendant of the boxes in the section on double-entry, now with assets listed above liabilities rather than the two side by side. The only other difference is that instead of the key balancing figures being the totals of assets and of liabilities, as they were in the boxes, the key balancing figures are now 'net assets' (= all assets less all liabilities) and 'shareholders' funds' (what the shareholders own outright). (These figures are the ones in bold, in the last column – **430**.) Total assets and total liabilities still balance, of course – at £785,000 if you add fixed and current assets or if you add current and long-term liabilities to shareholders' funds.

Note certain conventions:

★ The £000s along the top mean that all the figures in this sheet are in thousands of pounds.

★ Figures in brackets are 'negative' to the balance sheet. They are not negative in themselves. Confused? The creditors figure is (175). This means that the company owes £175,000 to various suppliers. This is a real, positive figure, but one that diminishes what the company owns (and increases what it owes) so is 'negative to the balance sheet'. Figures in brackets lower the key balancing figures (= 'net assets' and 'shareholders' funds', remember).

Futura Gadgets Ltd:
Balance Sheet as at 31st December 2006

	£000	£000	£000	£000
ASSETS				
Fixed Assets				
Land and buildings	200			
Plant and machinery	100			
Vehicles	15			
Office/factory fixtures and fittings	15			
				330
Current Assets				
Stocks (raw materials; work in progress;				
'finished' but unsold goods)	200			
Debtors (customers owing Futura money)	250			
Cash in deposit account		5		
			455	
LIABILITIES				
Current Liabilities (payable within one year)				
Bank loan and overdraft	(30)			
Creditors (suppliers to whom Futura				
owes money)	(175)			
			(205)	
'Net current assets'				
(= *Current Assets less Current Liabilities*)				250
Long-term Liabilities				
Mortgage on office and factory	(100)			
Bank loan	(50)			
				(150)
NET ASSETS (= *all* assets less *all* liabilities)				**430**
SHAREHOLDERS' FUNDS				
Share capital (injections of cash by owners)	225			
'Profit and loss account' (= accumulated				
profits ploughed back into the business				
over the years)	205			
				430

★ A column of figures with a line under it means that the column has to be added up (just as sums did at school). Just in case this gets too easy, convention places the answer in a later column (usually, but not always, the next column along). So we get:

$$
\begin{array}{r}
200 \\
250 \\
\underline{5} \\
455
\end{array}
$$

There is a reason for this: this leaves the sum to be used in a further calculation, as:

$$
\begin{array}{r}
455 \\
\underline{(205)} \\
250
\end{array}
$$

★ 'Bank loans' appear in both current and long-term liabilities. This is because a part of the loan will be repayable within the year, and the rest repayable later. Note also that the figure included for overdraft will be the amount currently outstanding, not the limit.

By far the best way to understand this material is to play around with the example. If you can, enter it on to a spreadsheet; if not, just alter the figures then redo the sums on paper. Imagine the company with £100,000 land and buildings, or no vehicles, or £50,000 of stock, or current liabilities of £60,000 (and so on…). Time spent doing this is time hugely well spent. That rather terrifying list of categories and those odd numbers in columns will suddenly become natural and obvious. Then you'll wonder why you never understood it, and feel sorry for those poor fools who can't even read a simple balance sheet…

Can we learn any instant lessons about Futura from its balance sheet?

It probably manufactures the gadgets, rather than just importing and selling them (or performing some kind of service based on them) – look at the amount of plant/machinery and stocks.

It is solvent: liabilities do not exceed assets.

Actually, it appears to have a nice portfolio of assets. This figure can be misleading, however. The portfolio could be even nicer: we don't know when the land or buildings were last valued. Or it could be less nice than it seems: if all the plant and machinery were old, they might be in need of (expensive) replacement – soon.

The company doesn't have a wonderful cash position, with £5,000 in a deposit account and an overdraft/short-term loan of more than that. But debtors exceed creditors by a healthy margin (250 to 175), which should mean this is not too serious. We'd want to check that all the debts owed to the company were likely to be paid.

We'd be keen to break down the stock figure, too, as it looks a bit high. Are there a lot of finished goods piling up? This might mean that the goods are no longer attractive to the marketplace. Trouble ahead for a once-successful company?

We say 'once-successful' as there is retained profit in the final, 'P and L' entry: a good sign.

Do we know from the balance sheet if Futura is currently trading profitably? No, we don't. Other tools are needed to tell us this (and are available – read on…).

The requirements of different sectors create very different-looking balance sheets, which is why we kicked off with a guess at what Futura does.

★ *Manufacturing companies* will have lots of fixed assets and reasonably high levels of stock. A key issue is not to waste these expensive assets through idleness.

★ *Retailers* will have a great deal of stock. Their key issue is to turn this stock over quickly (and, usually, profitably).

★ *Service businesses* will have 'small' balance sheets, with few assets plus stock in the form of work in progress – if they have a plutonium list of happy clients, this is an intangible asset which will not show up in the balance sheet. We would look carefully at the debtors figure for a service business (see below for more on this).

★ *Software companies*, like service businesses, will have few assets. Most of their early money goes on writing code, but they are not allowed to 'capitalise' this (by which we mean they can't put it in the balance sheet as an asset, the way Enron did with its future income flows). If the business is new, and has been unable to fund itself from revenue, it may also have a negative figure for 'profit and loss' (the final entry), funded by a large amount of debt, or, more likely, as lenders tend to fight shy of new software companies, 'share capital injected by owners'.

A term related to the balance sheet that readers will no doubt have heard is *working capital*. This is effectively the short-term funding you need for the 'engine room' of the business, and is contrasted with the long-term funding you need for the purchase of large fixed assets.

At the heart of every business is a wealth-creating cycle. Raw materials are ordered from suppliers. These are turned into finished products. People go out and sell these products. Customers place orders. Finally, the products are shipped out... Money flows round the system in a different way. Suppliers need to be paid. Usually money won't come in from customers until later: even if credit terms are the same from suppliers as for customers, the 'getting materials, making them into products and delivering them' part of the cycle takes time. A financial gap has opened here, which has to be filled by something.

For a company like Futura, with a lot of stock, this gap will be quite large.

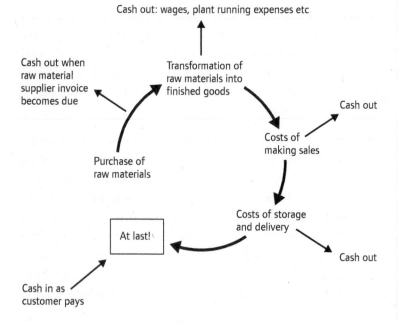

What fills the gap, of course, is money: the 'working capital' of the business. Most start-ups have to provide this themselves. Once the business is established, a bank overdraft is the preferred source. (More on the specifics of funding later.)

Note that, although the cycle depicted above is that of a manufacturing company like Futura, *all* businesses need working capital: retailers, software companies, even service companies. The latter are notoriously bad at collecting debt, probably because they don't feel that working capital matters as much to them as it does to their manufacturing counterparts (which it doesn't, until the company starts making a complete mess of it). We've heard service companies chase payments by saying: 'Er, we did some work for you three months ago… No, we're not sure how many days' work it was, now… Six, was it? Well, let's call it that…'

The working capital requirement of a company is never static; it grows as the company grows. So if the bank won't increase your overdraft but you are growing, you have a problem. In addition, the working capital requirement can suddenly skyrocket if:

★ A debtor defaults (even very late payment can cause severe problems)

★ The manufacturing process gets held up

★ A big order comes in, with no cash up front, leading to sudden large purchases of stock

Or, of course, if

★ The bank decides to call in the overdraft

Companies can go into liquidation because of working capital meltdowns, even if they have more fixed assets than liabilities.

But don't panic about this. Control of working capital is a standard skill of a finance cornerstone: the issue will be returned to later in the book.

The last item on the Futura balance sheet (profit and loss), and the question we asked earlier, about how the company is currently trading, both lead nicely into the other well-known financial information format…

The profit and loss account

The balance sheet represents a snapshot of the company. It is taken at a moment in time – in our example 31st December, or, more precisely, close of business on 31st December. The profit and loss account (or P and L) covers a period of time, usually a month for internal 'management' accounts and a year for official 'statutory' accounts. It asks: 'Have we made a profit over this period?'

Or, to expand, it asks … how much money did we invoice our customers for? How much did we spend on making what we sold? How much other expenditure did we incur just running the business? What about the taxman and dividends? Is there anything left?

Behind these lie more fundamental questions. 'Is our value-creation process efficient?' 'If not, where can we improve it?'

In theory, creating an account to model the first set of questions should be easy:

'How much money did we invoice our customers for?' is the start of the P and L: *turnover*, the amount of sales revenue (excluding VAT) earned – or at least, invoiced – during the year (or month, but for this example we'll imagine an annual account). Remember, this is *not* the same question as 'how much cash is actually coming into our account?' unless every customer pays you straight away.

'How much did we spend on making what we sold?' In the UK, this figure is called the *cost of sales*. It's not a good term because it is ambiguous: to the sales cornerstone 'cost of sales' means something totally different, the cost of making a sale – i.e. the salesperson's time, travel, the trip with the client to Amsterdam etc. We prefer the American term *Cost of Goods Sold*. Cost of Goods Sold is the cost of raw materials, the actual labour that went into making the items, the use of machines (electricity, wear and tear etc.), and other things *directly related* to the manufacture such as use of factory space and heating/lighting the factory.

Other costs incurred by the company are *indirect*.

There is, of course, an element of arbitrariness in what is directly related and what is indirect. Clearly some costs are totally indirect, such as the chairman's new office suite or the recent works outing to Blackpool. But what about the wages of the factory foreman? The cost of moving raw materials around the yard? To avoid confusion (and endless debates), the profession has worked out a series of rules to say what is 'direct', and can thus go into the Cost of Goods Sold figure, and what is indirect, and thus can't. If you want to take this further, consult the accountants' 'bible', *Preparing Company Accounts* by Ray Mayes (Editor), published by Croner CCH Group. But don't expend too much effort: later in this book we shall introduce another similar (but not quite the same) way of categorising costs.

On to the next of our questions…

How much other expenditure did we incur just running the business? Answer, of course, is all the indirect expenses. The suite; the trip to Blackpool; the sales, finance and marketing departments; delivery; the tea lady…

These indirect expenses are often referred to as *overheads*. The profession divides these into 'distribution costs' and 'administrative expenses', not a distinction we find massively useful.

What about the taxman and dividends? Is there anything left? This is at least self-explanatory, though the topic of taxation is a complex one, which we discuss later.

A model, simple profit and loss account is shown overleaf.

Futura Gadgets Ltd:
Profit and Loss Account for Year ended 31st Dec 2006

		£000
Turnover		1,600
Less: Cost of Goods Sold		(1,000)
Gross profit		600
Gross margin % (= gross profit/turnover)	37.5%	
Less: Other costs (overheads)		(520)
Net profit before tax		80
Net margin % (net profit before tax/turnover)	5.0%	
Less: Tax on profit		(15)
Net profit after tax		65
Less: Dividends paid and proposed		(40)
Profit retained in the business		
(transfer to this year's balance sheet)		**25**

Note the terms gross and net profit.

★ *Gross profit* tells you if your core 'wealth-creating cycle' of making things is efficient and/or cost-effective (it could be efficient but not cost-effective, if you were charging too little).

★ *Profit before tax* tells you if the business as a whole is actually making money (you could have an efficient, cost-effective wealth-creation cycle but too much fat in the back office). This is sometimes called 'net profit', but the term is a loose one. 'Net' just means 'with something taken out' (so when you hear a sum of money 'net of tax', it means what's left of an earlier, larger sum once the taxman has taken his slice). So the words 'net profit' are vague. Net of what? We like net of all costs, direct and indirect, as in the example above, but some people talk of 'net profit' and mean profit net of all costs *and* tax. Or net of costs, tax and dividends...

'Gross margin' and 'net margin' are ratios developed from the above. The term 'gross margin' is also often misused – we've heard people use it when they meant gross profit. Correctly, and we insist it be used correctly, it is gross profit divided by turnover, *expressed as a percentage*. So in the example above, it's $(600/1600) \times 100 = 37.5$ per cent.

You can imagine the confusion that reigns around the term 'net margin'. Or perhaps you'd rather not... We will use the term as profit before tax divided by turnover, expressed as a percentage. So the net margin here is $(80/1600) \times 100 = 5$ per cent.

Different industries have different standard levels of margin, so these two figures – hugely valuable when understood in the contexts of an industry sector and of the history of the particular business – don't tell us a huge amount on their own.

It's harder to read deep truths about a business from its P and L. Futura's thin net margin is not wonderful, but many manufacturing companies are trading at a paper loss, so they're not in disastrous trouble.

We'd like to know if the company is owner-managed: if it were, the poor net margin might be due to management extravagance: paying themselves excessive salaries, driving round in company Mercedes and staying at the George V when they go to meet Parisian customers. Of course, this is extravagance from an outsiders' perspective: for the owner/managers, they are getting what they want out of what is actually a nice, efficient business.

So, there we have the two classic means of delivering financial information, the balance sheet and the P and L.

Matching and depreciation

At this stage, we need to introduce two key technical (but actually not very complicated) terms.

Matching

Why do companies spend money? In theory (and, as often as possible, in practice) the answer is to make more money later. You buy a machine to make things you will sell. You buy a van to deliver them. Matching is the accounting principle that recognises this, insisting that expenditure by the company should be matched to the income generated as a result of that expenditure.

Remember that Futura included in its Cost of Goods Sold in 2006 'wear and tear' of the machines used in that year. In theory, they could have accounted for each machine in another way: by putting the total cost into the P and L account the day they bought it. Wouldn't this be more sensible? After all, once you've bought it and paid for it, it's here and the money is somewhere else...

But this would not reflect the reality that a tiny bit of the machine gets used up with each piece of work it does. Instead, it would make the profit figures in the P and L, especially gross profit, meaningless. Gross profit is supposed to tell you about the cost-efficiency of your wealth-creation cycle. If all the cost of one especially large machine were put into its first year, it would look as if the cycle became horribly inefficient for one year, then suddenly became efficient again. Instead, by matching the expenditure on each machine to the income it generates over time, we present a more realistic and useful picture.

Depreciation

This is how accountants put the matching principle into action. They depreciate an asset over the length of time that the owners expect to be using it (over its 'economic useful life', to use the technical term) by doing the following:

★ The asset is placed in the balance sheet when it is bought

★ The value is 'written down' over time, by taking a bit of that value and 'putting it through the P and L' every year.

Still foxed? An example will make things clear. If you buy a second-hand lathe for £4,000, you put it in the balance sheet as a fixed asset. How long do you plan to use it for? Four years? At the end of year one, you add £1,000 to the Cost of Goods Sold figure in the P and L, to reflect the wear and tear of the lathe in making that year's products. In the balance sheet you restate its value as £3,000 (this is called its 'net book value'). Next year you do the same – add another £1,000 to Cost of Goods Sold, to cover the cost of making *that* year's products, and put a new net book value in the year-end balance sheet of £2,000. And so on, until after four years the lathe is not mentioned in the balance sheet and is not being charged against turnover in the P and L. If you're still using it, it's generating pure profit. (And if you're not still using it, sell it!)

That is one way of depreciating assets, known as *straight-line* depreciation. *Reducing balance* depreciation writes the 'net book value' down by a fixed percentage, rather than a fixed amount, every year. If you depreciated the lathe by 25%, after year one it would be valued at £3,000 in the balance sheet, and you'd put £1,000 into Cost of Goods Sold in that year's P and L. After year two it would be valued at (£3,000 × 75% =) £2,250, and you'd put a cost of (£3,000 × 25% =) £750 through the P and L. After year three it's worth (£2250 × 75% =) £1687.50, and (£2250 × 25% =) £562.50 goes through the P and L. And so on.

The latter system (and the 25% figure) is used by the Inland Revenue, so most small businesses use it, to make submitting accounts to the Revenue easier.

Anything that costs over £500 and is expected to generate a flow of income over more than one year should be treated this way. You put it into the balance sheet as a 'fixed asset'; you write its value down over the years through 'Cost of Goods Sold' on the P and L.

Small asset purchases, under £500, should be treated as any other expense (like the heating bill or wages), and put through the P and L. It would be as absurd to put a £5 box of biros into the balance sheet and depreciate it over four years, even if the box lasted that long, as it would be to charge the purchase of a vast new machine to one year's profits. (However this did not stop one tax official, some years ago, trying to get Steve to write down a £25 book by the reducing balance method, as 'he was going to use it for more than one year'.)

Enron used to fiddle its P and L as well as its balance sheet. The firm called all sorts of costs that should have been charged to the year's P and L 'acquiring an asset', put that asset on the balance sheet and wrote it down very slowly, thus making a much less apparent dent in profits and puffing up the balance sheet.

Just to make the above distinction crystal clear...

Accounting for expenditure

| Purchase of Assets over £500 | Put straight in balance sheet as asset |
| | Charge to P and L over life of asset via depreciation |

▶▶

Purchase of small Assets	Charge to P and L at once
Bills, wages etc.	Charge to P and L at once
Purchase of raw materials	Put straight in balance sheet as 'stocks'
	Charge to P and L as used

Beermat.biz

Statutory accounts

By law, private company accounts have to be filed annually with Companies House, not more than ten months after your 'year-end' (see the chapter on tax for more on this innocuous-sounding notion). These accounts follow a specific format – which we don't want to discuss in great detail here: a model set, plus explanations of the technical terms that inevitably accompany such a document, are reproduced in Appendix A. For now, note that statutory accounts consist of:

★ Directors' report

★ P and L account

★ Balance sheet

★ Notes on the above

Based on a rather complex set of criteria (details available from Companies House at www.companieshouse.gov.uk), small companies are exempt from submitting their P and L and have to submit fewer notes. This is useful a) as it saves work, and b) because it stops nosey competitors finding out details such as your level of turnover.

Finally, note that though *audits* have to be done by registered auditors ('the profession'), you can and should prepare and submit your own statutory accounts.

The problem with statutory accounts is that many people think that they are what accounting is 'all about' for the start-up or SME. Do these, and you have 'done the accounts'. No, you have done some accounts, and fulfilled a legal obligation. You have not told the entrepreneur/owner/team everything they need to know about the financial performance of their business! What else you need to know follows in Chapter Five.

We have reached the end of this survey of the very basics. All non-accountants should now be happy to look at a balance sheet or a P and L, and be familiar with the following terms: single and double entry books, assets (fixed, current, intangible, 'net current' and net), liabilities (current and long-term), share capital, shareholders' funds, creditors, debtors, turnover, Cost of Goods Sold, cost of sales, gross profit, profit before tax, gross and net margin, matching, depreciation and statutory accounts. If any of these still baffle you, go back and remind yourself.

Happy with all the above? Great, let's get the business moving!

Chapter Three: The Seedling Business

So you've got this great idea…

This chapter deals with the very early life of the idea, when you are effectively testing out whether it really has what it takes, or just sounds good. We call this the seedling phase. This phase ends either in 'nice try: back to the pub, let's think of another idea', or in the idea making a transition to a proper business with real (but still, of course, unrealised) potential.

A finance cornerstone is of use from the very start. Even when your idea is just words, a chat over a beer with a finance specialist can be of huge value. Once you look like making your first sale, the need for a finance cornerstone begins to increase, and it builds from then on. However if you don't know anyone who will fulfil this role, or if you are so strapped for cash that £250 a day seems a fortune, you can get by without a finance cornerstone for a while. Fine, but be aware that your need will grow. By the time you are ready to make the transition to the next phase, you must have someone to carry out this role.

But back to the very start … the 'Original Beermat' of elevator pitch, mentor and potential first customer needs to be filled in.

Then (for lucky businesses that start with teams rather than lone entrepreneurs) everyone goes away and 'has a think about it': the potential sales cornerstone chatting to a few friends in the business, a potential technical cornerstone rattling up a prototype in the garden shed. If the finance cornerstone is there at this very early stage, what do they do?

★ They could get together with the operations cornerstone and do some sums about manufacture/delivery.

★ They may well have a range of useful contacts. Potential customers or mentors, perhaps. Or someone with a potentially complementary product/service. Or, of course, potential rivals – what mistakes have they made? Get talking to these contacts, informally of course.

★ Most important of all, they will immediately start pondering a financial Magic Question – 'How will this make money?' The answer to this is through a *business model*. The business model is often the creation of the finance cornerstone: even when it is the entrepreneur's, it is the ultimate responsibility of the finance cornerstone to think the model through, test it and amend it if necessary.

The business model

The term can scare people off, as it sounds business-schooly and abstract. It isn't: it's simply what it says, a model of the business, showing how it will work. Imagine a working model of an early steam engine, with jiggling pistons, flywheels whirring round and smoke puffing out of a chimney. This model is composed of certain specific units, assembled in a particular way to transmute one thing (fuel) into another (motion). A *business* model is no different (okay, it doesn't have smoke coming out of it): an assembly of processes designed to turn one thing (customer needs) into another thing (profit).

There are three main components to a business model: the vision, the story and the pay-off.

1. The vision. This should have been outlined in the elevator pitch. Where's the pain? (More specifically, in what segment of the market is the pain, and what exactly does the pain consist of?) What are we going to do about it? Why should our target market buy from us rather than someone else?

2. The story. The vision asked what we were going to do to solve the pain, and its answer was general ('we're going to provide full-service software for vets' 'we're going to provide fair trade clothing' etc.). Here it becomes specific, answering the question 'how will we do this?'

3. The pay-off. How will we make money from doing the above?

The last of these three is the area where a finance cornerstone can add most value, but it's worth looking at the first two from a financial perspective as well...

The vision. This should be the creation of the entrepreneur, but often isn't. The entrepreneur has a gut feeling that something is being done badly and could be done many times better (or quicker, or cheaper, or nicer for the customer). A finance person is often the one to pin the entrepreneur down to specifics.

The story. How are we going to make the vision a reality? This breaks down into two main sections, making what you provide (sourcing and manufacture of things; delivery and support of a service) and selling it (sales and marketing; distribution of things).

★ Sourcing and manufacturing. The operations cornerstone should know what he or she is doing – but have they costed accurately? The answer is almost undoubtedly a) no and b) it doesn't yet matter that much, as things will change anyway.

However it's never too early for the finance cornerstone to get a handle on the costs of key sourcing and production processes.

★ Service delivery and support. The same applies.

★ Sales. Have a sales model that stresses person-to-person sales, as these drive most start-ups.

★ Marketing. The traditional questions of the 'marketing mix'. How will the customer find out about us? How will they buy: when, where, in what amounts, at what price? If the finance cornerstone has sector experience, they may be an expert on this. Even if not, he or she should be working out what prices will work for the business (see the notion of Break-Even Point later).

★ Distribution. The finance cornerstone should be costing the various means.

Note that the three 'selling it' sections are all linked. How you distribute depends partially on how customers want to buy (online? From a shop? etc.), as does how you sell…

The pay-off. This is where a finance cornerstone comes into their own. Remember, again, the McDonalds story, where the foil turned Ray Kroc's excellent busy-ness into a great business. Where does the business actually make its money?

Don't just think of one revenue stream. There may be several. eBay, for example, charge fees for joining, fees for advertising, and a commission on sales. Insurance companies don't just make money on premiums but from sitting on cash (as premiums are paid in advance). Some companies make small margins on sales and bigger money from hidden user charges, for example selling items cheap by post, then adding a hefty 'post and packaging' charge. Many businesses – this is very much in the Beermat spirit

– sell physical objects cheap, and make their money on the services, training and consultancy associated with these objects.

Go back to the Magic Question, 'Where's the pain?' Pain is rarely assuaged by delivering a 'thing' (grommet, CD full of software etc.), but by a whole 'pain-relieving' service. This could consist of initial consultancy about the problem, creating and providing a solution (including physically producing things), instructing people how to best use the things, monitoring their use, introducing modifications as circumstances change... All of these are potential revenue sources; in practice some of them will be and others won't. Consider where in the story of pain relief (a story which business-school types call a 'value chain') money can be made. It's most likely to be where you deliver something special, personal, unique. Concentrate on that. Where competition is fierce (often in the manufacture of things and in the transport of things from A to B) money is unlikely to be made. Can you outsource these bits of the 'value chain' to someone else?

As well as the above, a finance cornerstone should develop an idea of the kind of 'financial shape' the business will have. What might its balance sheet, P and L and cash flow look like? Will it have lots of fixed assets and/or stock, and, if so, how will it finance them? What kind of margins (gross and net) will it be earning? At the moment, you can't be too specific about these, but look around at other businesses solving the same pain, and take an intelligent guess.

Setting up a basic accounting system

Do this from the very start. If there is no finance person on the team, the most methodical of you should keep the books (the system we outline below is very simple). If you are a lone entrepreneur, then you must keep these books (and if you remain a sole trader, you can keep on using this system for ever).

The system consists of an 'Analysed Cashbook' plus two spreadsheets, of invoices raised and of invoices received.

The Analysed Cashbook is just a list of all payments in to and out of the business. In the example below, the new company buys £6,000 worth of raw materials (and has to pay VAT on top of that). It makes them into a product, and sells them for £10,000 + VAT, cash on delivery. The cost of effecting the delivery is £1,000 + VAT.

The company has £3,525 in the bank as a result of these transactions. Of this, £525 will be payable to the VATman at the end of the quarter.

Analysed Cashbook

Item No.	Date	Ref.
1	31/01/06	Chq 00
2	15/03/06	BACS
3	15/03/06	Chq 00

Customer Invoices

Invoice No.	Date
01bi01	28/01/06
02di01	28/03/06

The Ref column would include paying-in slip numbers.

The Cost of Goods Sold and overheads columns can be broken down into sub-categories, depending on what your main costs are. For example overheads could be 'Staff wages, travel and subsistence, rent, utilities, telephone, others'.

The list of customer invoices is simple.

Note that a good format for invoice numbers is:

sequential invoice number/letters to identify customer name/ sequential customer invoice number

So if the next invoice raised was to Bibblethwaite then the invoice number would be 03bi02 (i.e. our third invoice, and our second to Bibblethwaite...).

The total of the last column of the customer invoice list is, of

Total In/(out) Inc. VAT	VAT	Total In/(out) Ex. VAT	Sales	Cost of Goods Sold	Overheads	Current Cash Balance
(7,050)	(1,050)	(6,000)		(6,000)		(7,050)
11,750	1,750	10,000	10,000			4,700
(1,175)	(175)	(1,000)			(1,000)	3,525

Customer	Total In/(out) Ex. VAT	VAT	Total In/(out) Inc. VAT	Date Paid	Amount Paid	Amount Outstanding
Bibblethwaite	10,000	1,750	11,750	15/3/06	11,750	—
Digtock	2,000	350	2,350	—	—	2,350

course, what would be put in your balance sheet as 'debtors' if one were to be drawn up at that moment.

The details for date and amount paid should agree with the Analysed Cashbook.

The list of supplier invoices received should be similar – though some small businesses call this ledger the 'in tray' and never formally note them, waiting till the supplier phones up to do anything about them. We recommend a more methodical and formal approach.

Culture

Great companies have great cultures. As a start-up, this may not seem to matter, but it does. It's never too early to start.

Culture is a huge subject, worthy of a book on its own. In this book, we will stick to the financial aspects of culture, and especially to two mindsets that will be essential to the company throughout its life.

If you are an entrepreneur, read the following section with extra care. If you are a finance cornerstone, you should know this stuff – your battle will be to make sure it gets into the DNA of the company.

The mindsets are 'think cash' and 'stay flexible'.

Mindset one: think cash

Most people think that successful business is about profit. This is clearly true, but it is even more helpful to think that a successful business is about cash. Profit is in a sense an arbitrary thing, determined in part by the conventions governing how you draw up your P and L, such as depreciation rates. Cash, on the other hand, is cash. The cleverest accountant in the world can't make cash appear from a set of accounts when there isn't any (they can, of course, help that business find cash, but that's different). Small (and not so small) businesses go under because of lack of cash, not because of lack of profit.

Some sensible 'think cash' rules to have in the business from day one...

Make payment conditions a central part of your position when negotiating deals, not just an afterthought. We're against the giving of discounts, unless there's something given back in return – like good payment terms. If the sales cornerstone negotiates a not-very-good deal in terms of price, but the cash comes in fast, they've not failed but done quite a good job. Tell them (and everyone else) so. On the other hand, if the payment terms are terrible, can you afford to do the deal at all?

The logical conclusion of this is to get the sales cornerstone to ask for cash up front. In some sectors, mainly those where undifferentiated, long-lasting goods are sold (and thus, if the customer doesn't pay, the vendor can reclaim the product and sell it elsewhere) they'll be very lucky to get this: the best that a salesperson can insist on is good payment terms. But in other sectors, this can work. Mike, for example, insists on payment up front for all his speaking work, and clients accept this, as speakers can't go round their audience reclaiming their words if the client doesn't pay up.

'Did you ask for cash up front, and what did they say?' is a good question for start-up entrepreneurs and finance cornerstones to be asking sales cornerstones.

Invoice as soon as possible. Sounds obvious, but many, many small firms don't do this. If you can invoice the moment the deal is agreed, perfect. If not, do so the moment after delivery. Right at the start of the company's life, the entrepreneur should take it upon him or herself to sit down every evening and ask, 'Have we sent out all our invoices?' Later on you will set up a formal system for this, which we describe in Chapter Six. Right now, just get it done!

Chase up invoices the moment they become due. Don't feel this is rude: it's proper business practice. Many small firms operate a policy of not paying till chased. (Many big firms are even worse, but chase them anyway.)

Be prepared to walk away from bad payers. If payers are predictably late, that's a pain but tolerable, as long as you know they are a stable business. What you don't want is a debtor going bust. Sudden lengthening of payment time can be a sign that this is imminent. Watch out for other signs (invoices suddenly paid with personal cheques, changes in previously stable order patterns), and make sure the networkers in your team are listening out for any rumours. If in doubt, no more supplies till they pay what they owe, and cash up front from then on.

Bank online. Some entrepreneurs are unhappy with this: they like to sign all the cheques going out and to watch the bookkeeper heading off to the bank before 3.30 with the day's incoming cheques. This is understandable, but it is not 'thinking cash'.

When you get cheques, take them to the bank the day they arrive. The odd customer will insist on paying the old-fashioned way. So make sure their cheques get paid in at once. Otherwise it's amazing how soon cheques start loitering in in-trays…

Should you *delay payment of your suppliers' invoices* as long as possible? We say no. Beermat companies are ethical, and we think you should follow the golden rule of 'do as you would be done by'. There's also a practical benefit to this: if you hit a cash crisis, a supplier who has been regularly paid by you is more likely to cut you some slack.

In practice, small businesses will have bill-paying sessions every week or every fortnight, when invoices that have become due get paid.

Keep all the books up to date. Again, the lone entrepreneur can often slip up here. Don't. Get yourself a finance cornerstone as soon as possible, but, until then, you have to do this stuff.

Do a regular cash-flow forecast. Right at the start of the business's life, this may be very speculative – but get used to doing it. See Chapter Five for a model.

Thinking cash is also a valuable mindset in big business – readers of *Beermat Entrepreneur* will recall the advice of Mike's mentor Sir Campbell Fraser (former president of the CBI and chairman of Dunlop and Scottish TV): 'Watch the cash, laddie'.

Mindset two: stay flexible

This is particularly important in these early stages, as you don't know whether the idea will really make it as a business or not. So don't spend money that you won't get back. As the business grows, this axiom remains important, as you never know when you are going to hit a downturn or obstacle of some kind.

Sadly, most entrepreneurs think the opposite, and love to acquire assets. Assets are seen as signs of *success* – as in the classic cartoon of the self-made man pointing to a huge factory and proudly telling his son, 'Some day, my boy, this will all be yours' (by which he means 'Look how well I've done, son!').

Assets are also perceived as being *secure*. 'If things go wrong, we can always sell the x…'

Both perceptions are illusions. In the first case yes, the old man's assets probably were a sign of success, built up over many years of successful business. A start-up's assets are paid for by the team, loans or angel money, and are not a sign of success but of being able to get money off people. The start-up entrepreneur can only say, 'Some day, my boy, this will all be yours – if the idea takes off, and provided the company doesn't fall into a cash hole, and…'

However that illusion, which most people see through easily, is harmless compared to the second one, that assets = security. This is much more insidious: it's equally untrue, but more generally believed. Assets do not equal security; a healthy balance sheet (lots owned, little owed) does.

Many assets like machines, computers, office furniture have incredibly low resale value. Land and property do not, but it's too early in the life of the company to be owning these, unless you plan to deal in them, or have a hidden agenda of being a property company (a wheeze employed by some franchisors: buy places, stick franchisees in them, charge them rents, pay the mortgages with these…).

The point is that you need to be able to take out costs if you hit a cash crisis. You can't do this if you've bought the asset: either you have spent cash on it which should have been kept for working capital, or you have borrowed to buy it and are stuck with monthly payments. If you hire the asset, you can take it back to the hirer at once (make sure you're not locked into a long-term contract). Yes, hiring can be more costly than other ways of getting the use of assets, but the added flexibility makes it worth doing.

You should understand the basic ways of hiring:

★ Machinery can be hired from places like HSS – look under 'Hire Services' in Yellow Pages, or 'Plant Hire' if you need some serious Tonka toys. You stipulate how long you want the item for (the minimum is a day, the maximum 'as long as you need it'). You may not even need to pay a deposit if the hirer can take credit card details.

★ Vehicles and photocopiers are usually *leased* via what is called an 'operating lease'. Lease periods are longer than hires. In both hire arrangements and operating leases, the hirer is responsible if the item malfunctions in any way, not you.

★ Some kinds of lease allow you to purchase the asset after a fixed period of time. Don't worry about this now: just get use of what you need, in decent condition, as cheaply as possible. When the idea takes off and becomes a business, you can revisit leasing and hire arrangements.

Of course, some assets don't even need to be hired. Right at the start, can you borrow what you need off friends? We don't mean money, but everything else.

Work from home, rather than finding an office.

Later on, we will develop the flexibility theme via the notions of fixed versus variable costs, but for now, keep it simple. 'Don't buy, hire. Or borrow.'

Basic financial culture on a Beermat

Think cash

★ Make payment terms a central part of your negotiations, not an afterthought

★ Try asking for cash up front

★ Send out invoices at once

★ Chase invoices when due

★ Bank online

★ Payments received in cheque or cash – take to the bank that day

★ Be ethical in paying supplier invoices

★ Do a regular cash-flow forecast

Stay flexible

★ Avoid the false lure of assets

★ Don't buy, hire

★ (in the seedling business) Borrow

Beermat.biz

Giving the business an identity

Early on in its life, in our view once the first sale has been made, the business needs to undergo two key processes that create an identity for it: formal registration and the setting up of a proper business bank account.

Others disagree. Many sole traders never get round to either of the above, and have perfectly good businesses doing all sorts of things from reflexology to trading First World War memorabilia on eBay with no registered company or special bank account. But for entrepreneurs and teams with bigger plans, now is the time to up your level of commitment and become official.

Note that serial entrepreneurs may well have a company through which they run all their ideas until any given idea takes off, at which point they give the new business its own identity. Mike's own 'Piglet Productions' was once a mobile disco, complete with seven-inch vinyl 45s (remember them?) and a home-made bubble machine, but has incubated many business ideas since then. This is fine, but must be seen as a transition. After a few sales, the business must become its own entity – and all cash from those early sales must be put into its own accounts.

If you have a finance cornerstone, make them responsible for these two tasks.

Task one: making it legal

The *Limited Company* is the best form for small but ambitious businesses. There are tax advantages, especially when you are not paying dividends, which you won't be to start with. It looks more professional. It's easier to administer, especially as you are growing.

An alternative that is growing in popularity is the *Limited Liability Partnership*, but we find this adds little value, while being harder to administer than the traditional Limited Company, especially when adding team members or subtracting them if they want out.

Either way, of course, you get that valuable limited liability. Sadly (except to lawyers) the world is becoming ever more litigious: those responsible for limited companies or LLPs cannot be sued for what their business does, unless they have acted unlawfully or provided personal guarantees, whereas partners in old-style partnerships and sole traders can be sued.

Setting up a limited company is not difficult. You can do it via the net – there are online registration agents offering formation for as little as £35 (for which you get all the documentation in electronic form: spend another £35 and you get hard copies). Or, if you prefer to act through an individual, go to a traditional, offline registration agent – look one up in Yellow Pages under 'Company Formation' if you don't know any. They shouldn't charge more than £100.

You need to provide some information.

★ the names of the director(s) and the company secretary

★ their addresses, dates of birth and details of other directorships held in last five years

★ some personal authentication details

★ your intended registered office

★ the names of the founder shareholders

★ personal authentication details for them

★ the authorised share capital

★ a brief description of what the company will do

★ your choice of company name

Looking at the above list in more detail:

The *company secretary* is a formal post, which can be filled by a director as long as there is more than one director in the business. The post involves:

★ organising general meetings of shareholders and ensuring that these are carried out according to company law.

★ maintaining a list of shareholders (the share register) and providing certificates for the shareholders.

★ submitting the annual statutory accounts (or 'abbreviated accounts' if turnover is less than £5.6 million) and the annual return, a form sent every year by Companies House asking for confirmation of certain details such as the identities of shareholders and directors.

★ informing Companies House if there is a change of director, address or share capital.

Many start-ups hire solicitors to do this work, at great expense. A finance cornerstone will charge much less. Modern company secretary work is not arduous: much of the submitting of data can now be done over the internet. Note, however, that there are stiff penalties for failing to submit the relevant material. These penalties fall on all the directors, so the company secretary won't be popular if he or she forgets. But the finance cornerstone should be the most organised person in the business, so they won't forget.

Make sure that all relevant communication gets to the company secretary. We know many start-ups where it gets put in a horrible-official-looking-stuff' pile and left there.

Plans are afoot to change the law so that small businesses no longer need a company secretary. Fine – but someone will still have to do the above jobs, and a finance cornerstone will still be the ideal person.

Personal authentication details are things like people's eye colour and mother's maiden name. This rather tedious extra chore is connected with fighting terrorism and money-laundering, so can't be waved away, however silly it seems. It's best to have the relevant people present when you file, so you can get these details from them.

The *registered office* must be a real address to which summonses can be served and where people can come and inspect documents if necessary. It does not have to be your trading address: many small businesses use their accountants or lawyers. However we are preaching early independence from the professions, so suggest that if you have a working office then that should also be your formal registered office.

Changing your registered office is easy: simply inform Companies House (this can be done online, free). The most difficult bit is probably moving the plate that you have to put up outside your registered office. The plate does not have to be brass, by the way. (Shame, really. We rather like them...)

You decide your own *authorised share capital*. A common format is that the company is divided into 1000 shares of £1 each, but this doesn't mean you have to start the business with £1000 – it's another formality. Neither do you have to allocate all the shares on day one. If only five shares are owned in the 1000 share company, one by each founding team member, as long as nobody owns the other 995, then they each own 20% of the company. (This apparently odd way of doing things makes it legally easier to issue more shares in the future.)

Each shareholder must put £1 into the business to pay for their shares, a ritual that must be followed.

Keep your *description of what the company will do* general. You will get back a 'Memorandum of Association' that restates this, and also allows you to do all sorts of other things. FDUK's memorandum entitles Steve and Jeff to (amongst other things) 'erect, construct, lay down, enlarge, alter and maintain roads, railways, tramways, sidings, bridges, reservoirs and shops'. Why? We have no idea.

Finally, your *choice of name*… Gone are the days when it was cheaper to get names off the shelf. Now you (or your agent) just go online, type in your chosen name, and, unless there's a good reason for you not to have it, it's yours. 'Good reasons' are largely that someone else has got there first, or that the name is 'sensitive', which either means rude or on a rather bizarre list (you can download it from www.companieshouse.gov.uk) of specially ring-fenced names.

All the above information will be sent to Companies House, the government body responsible for registering and keeping records of businesses. They will then get back to you (via the registration agent) with:

★ a Certificate of Incorporation

★ a company registration number

★ a book of blank share certificates

★ your Memorandum of Association

★ your Articles of Association

The Memorandum of Association states what the company is called, where it's based and what it does (including all the fanciful stuff about enlarging tramways).

The Articles of Association are the rules for running the company's internal affairs: ownership, borrowing powers and practice for general meetings and for getting rid of directors.

We believe that the latter should be extended via a formal *shareholder agreement*, though in law all you need are the Articles of Association. The shareholder agreement should:

★ set out the procedure if a shareholder wants out

★ protect dependants' rights if a shareholder dies

★ set out procedures for settling stalemates

★ protect minority shareholders in case of the majority deciding to sell (usually the minority have the right to sell at the same price the majority are getting)

★ protect majority shareholders against minorities who become bolshy, for example refusing to sell to a majority-agreed buyer (the minority have to sell)

For an extra fee, the registration agent will also provide a company seal. This has not been mandatory since 1989, however (another blow against surrealism in the workplace!).

Finally, note that there are rules about what information a Limited Company has to put on its communications. Detailed information is available from Companies House, but in essence all business letters and order forms must bear the name of the company (in a legible form); its country of registration (England, Wales, Scotland, Northern Ireland); its registered number; and the address of its registered office. When you register for VAT, a delightful subject we will cover in the next chapter, you have to quote your VAT number on invoices.

Task two: a company bank account

Many entrepreneurs resist this. They like the feeling that their name is on the account, and probably think business bank accounts are a rip-off, having heard horror stories of overcharging. We disagree.

Firstly, the deal for business banking is actually very good. Banks often waive charges for the first two years, as they want your business. Is it really worth soldiering on with an inappropriate banking set-up just to save some money in two years' time?

Secondly, a proper business account makes you look more professional. When a customer asks 'Who do want the cheque made payable to?', you should reply 'Bloggsbiz Ltd', not 'Fred Bloggs no 3 account' or, even worse, 'Er, um, which account is most overdrawn at the moment? Just let me call my wife...' Similarly, suppliers will prefer to deal with a properly set up account.

Thirdly, overcharging is a bit of a myth. We have encountered very few problems with this. Companies that get into furious rows with banks about years of overcharging tend to be ones where finance is a low priority. If you don't monitor your finances properly, errors can creep in and then multiply – a small mistake nudges an account into the red; cheques start to bounce, incurring more charges (and so on). The finance cornerstone should always check bank charges, and question anything that seems wrong *at once*. It will almost always be sorted out quickly (and in the rare cases where it is not, the finance cornerstone will know how to escalate the problem within the bank until it is sorted).

Small businesses, used to giving personal customer service, don't really understand how banks work. Banks are vast organisations – go and look at the HQ of a major bank if you want to see how vast (the HSBC building in Docklands is a good example: it reaches halfway to the sky, and they use the whole thing. And they've got another, even bigger, one in Hong Kong.) Being this vast, they work by rules. That does not mean that they are totally inflexible, but if left to their own devices they will follow automated patterns, which in turn cause 'tiny error that grows into a calamity' scenarios like the one above. Your bank manager will have hundreds of business accounts to manage, and this means that he or she will 'manage by exception' – if you are ticking along within agreed limits, you will be ignored; if you overstep a limit, an alarm bell will ring and the manager will get involved. Hence the comment 'they're only interested in bad news', which is not fair. 'They only have time to firefight' is nearer the truth.

Don't forget that your bank manager, however powerful they may look behind their grand desk in their smart office, is actually a cog in an immense machine. They have a boss to report to, who is looking for lots of smooth-running accounts and as few problems as possible (and who, in turn, has a boss to report to...). So help them look good!

The fourth reason for getting a proper business bank account is that the account separates the business from the entrepreneur. The business will always be, up to a point, an extension of their personality, but it also needs to be a separate legal and commercial entity. Having its own bank account reinforces this.

Do shop around when looking for a bank. The two key criteria are personal recommendation from someone in a similar situation to yourself, and whether the finance cornerstone likes the person you will be dealing with. Don't waste time comparing the minutiae of the different banks' offers: they all tend to be very similar, and anyway will be different (in suitably trivial ways) next month. Find a person you like and trust, and build a business relationship with them.

Just as we recommend not buying any assets when you start, don't incur any liabilities by asking for money from the bank at once. 'It's like asking someone to sleep with you on the first date,' comments one bank manager we know. Start by putting in founders' money (the original share capital). If you can, do this slowly, not all at once: if you're committed to putting in £20,000, put in £5,000 a month. Banks love regularity. Once the account has been running for a while and things are clearly going well – that's the time to ask for money.

Note that finance cornerstones are the best people to conduct meetings with the bank. Not entrepreneurs. Entrepreneurs and bank managers are usually cut from very different cloth: enthusiastic versus sceptical, mould-breaking versus cautious, big-picture versus detail-minded. If you have a finance cornerstone who can choreograph the meeting, so the entrepreneur pops in briefly, charms the manager and then disappears – perfect!

Other administration

Try and keep this to a minimum this early on in the life of the business. You may need some 'infrastructure' for the delivery of early sales, but make it as simple as possible.

For example, you will need company notepaper, business cards and a standard invoice form. Make sure that the latter has your bank account details and payment terms on it, nice and clear so that late payers don't have the excuse of ignorance.

When you have assembled your founding team of five people, it will be necessary to investigate stakeholder pensions, a topic we discuss later in the chapter on tax and law.

Seedling funding

Initial funding should come from the team, in the form of cash and 'sweat equity' (work done for nothing).

Then, as soon as possible, revenue. If your idea really does offer to solve customer pain, can you get money up front for it? 'Early adopter' customers should help you develop the product/service, too. This attitude lies at the heart of the Beermat approach.

Other people may want to chip in. Friends, family and fans of the business (the latter are really early angels). Three Fs. (Another version of the Three Fs is 'friends, family and fools', but we wouldn't advise being that cynical.) The problem of friends/

family money is that it can come with emotional strings attached – not usually a good thing. Will the friendship survive if the business doesn't?

Banks may lend you money – but you will probably have to provide a personal guarantee. Do you really want to put your house on the line? Banks are also wary about granting overdrafts to start-ups. They want to know that your business has got off the ground before lending it money. We agree with them: get your business moving yourself.

Some start-ups may be eligible for *grants*. The Prince's Trust (www.princes-trust.org.uk) helps young people. The DTI, through Regional Development Authorities, offers various grants. Selective Finance for Investment (SFI) grants are for new projects in 'assisted' areas, and there are different types of grant for technology development. Rather than go into these in depth, we suggest you contact your local Business Link about these, a) because the grants change pretty regularly and b) because local advisors will have local information.

Two points to note ... first, the schemes (and the business assistance systems generally) differ in England, Scotland, Wales and Northern Ireland. Second, and most important, most grants tend to be for existing businesses, not brand-new start-ups. As a result of the latter, we will say a little more on them in later sections.

The *Small Firms Loan Guarantee* is also available for start-ups, though as with grants, its preferred destination is existing businesses eager to expand, so we will discuss it later. Prove your idea before tapping into this hugely valuable resource.

Finally, NESTA (the National Endowment for Science, Technology and the Arts) is a kind of miniature, benevolent venture capitalist (if such a thing can be imagined), funded by the National Lottery. If you have a particularly creative or high-tech idea, check them out on www.nesta.org.uk

Some comments on funding different types of start-up:

Software. This type of business often has high start-up costs, as lots of code has to be written before anything saleable appears. You can mitigate this by offering equity to code-writers. Grants for product development may also be available.

Retail. You'll probably have to fund the fixtures and fittings yourself. Suppliers may help with favourable terms on stock – they want you to be an outlet for them.

Seedling funding on a Beermat

Requirement:	Funded by:
Basic set-up costs, 'pure seed capital'	Entrepreneur, cornerstones
	Revenue as soon as possible
Working capital	ditto
Early, necessary work	Do it yourselves!
Any fixed assets you have to buy	Don't buy any!
Stock (for retailer)	Get excellent terms from supplier
Any promotion, PR	Get it free!

Beermat.biz

Manufacturing. You're unlikely to avoid borrowing, but strive to keep it to a minimum. Hire, don't buy: this applies to everything except computers. If you really must buy, buy second-hand – there are second-hand markets in most machinery, from local auctions to eBay. Finance this purchase with a loan secured on the asset. A DTI grant may be available too – check – but it won't cover the whole cost.

Do have a think: 'Are we really a manufacturing company, or a sales, distribution and service company?' In other words, can we outsource the manufacturing part of the story?

Service. No need for external funding. Get revenue coming in at once!

The White Paper

Note that once your first customer has been well served (or, if your product is some kind of long-term contract, once the contract is up and running smoothly), you should write a White Paper on the success of the sale. This is a version of the business model, especially the 'story' section – though this time, it's for real. What did we actually do, what did the client love/hate (etc.)?

One function of the White Paper is as a sales document: 'We delighted XYZ plc; let us delight you…' If you can *quantify* that delight – 'we saved them £10,000 in six weeks' – then that adds huge power to your sales pitch. XYZ are unlikely to volunteer this information, but a finance cornerstone should be able to work out a rough estimate by asking a few innocent-sounding questions about costs, looking at what you actually delivered, doing some sums and finally bouncing a figure off the happy customer. 'So we must have saved you around £10,000…'. Watch the customer's immediate reaction: unless they're master poker players, they'll be unable to prevent some response that will tell if the guess is too high, too low, or on target.

The finance cornerstone should also do a quick audit of the sale, to check how much things cost and how much less they could be got for next time. The first run at anything almost always costs more than later iterations (unless the later versions are radically different): items are purchased that turn out to be unnecessary, components are overspecified, you suddenly find a new supplier who's 10% cheaper (and so on…).

Even if your sale is quite small-scale (the example above comes from the IT services industry), it's worth running through the above processes.

On to the next phase

Even one sale is a big leap – many bright ideas don't even get this far. You have a *product*, a genuine market offer, not just an idea. You do not yet have much of a business – but you soon will have, as long as further sales follow, which they should.

Sell and deliver some more, always keeping an eye on customer pain and how you solve it. Your product will probably be developing fast, and the finance cornerstone needs to be keeping a close eye on these changes. Are things proving to be more expensive than planned? Undoubtedly. Are you able to command the price you hoped? Possibly not. Or maybe you can add something you didn't understand at the outset, and ask loads more… Is the market quite what you thought it would be? Unlikely.

Great. You're learning and your offer is changing to meet the market. There should soon come a moment when you feel confident that the two dovetail well enough to generate good numbers of regular sales.

You've got a business!

And, of course, a whole new set of challenges, which we will discuss in Chapter Six. But first, we need to look at more technical material…

Chapter Four: Tax and the law

Tax

Any book on finance runs up against the problem that the rules are always changing. Nowhere is this more true than when discussing tax. No doubt by the time this book appears in the shops, something will have changed since we sent the manuscript to the publisher.

Another problem when writing about tax is that the system is complicated: this book is designed to give an overview, for an entrepreneur keen to know what a finance cornerstone should do, or as a checklist for a finance cornerstone. There is not the space to go into the tax system in depth, any more than we would go into the precise aetiology of every illness in a general book on health. (If you think this is wrong, just think of all those trees that have been saved from pulping as a result...)

However the good news is that the basic structure of the system is unlikely to change, and the basic principles of handling tax won't change at all.

The most important thing about taxation is not to panic. Yes, you do have to calculate your own liability for tax and pay it, and yes, the Inland Revenue will check if it suspects you have seriously miscalculated, either deliberately or by mistake. But the

Revenue has better things to do than check that seedling and sapling businesses have submitted perfect accounts. So do your best, and don't try and cheat. (If you cheat, you might get away with it; but if you get spotted, investigated and caught, the Revenue has a memory like an elephant and will scrutinise your accounts for ever.) File and pay on time, partly because you get fined if you don't, but also because late payers are more likely to be investigated, which is a tedious distraction, even if you have done things by the book. Finally, if you get stuck, ask for help from a tax specialist.

If you keep to these rules, you'll have little trouble from taxation, apart from the hassle of doing it – something which is much reduced by computerised accounts.

Dealing with the Revenue on a Beermat

★ Don't panic!

★ Don't cheat

★ Computerise your accounts

★ File on time

★ Pay on time

★ If you get stuck, ask a tax specialist

◖Beermat.biz

Your encounter with the Inland Revenue – or HM Revenue & Customs (HMRC) as it is now called, having recently merged with Customs and Excise – will begin early. Every company has to give written notice to Revenue & Customs within 3 months of starting to trade. Once notice has been given, Revenue & Customs will issue a notice to file a return, generally with a copy of the corporation tax return form (Form CT600).

From then on, the Revenue is never far in the background. We'll be looking at the four main ways the Chancellor gets his mitts on your (and your employees') hard-earned money – but first of all…

Your year-end

Every business has to have a year-end, when it draws up annual accounts. Futura Gadgets, in the Chapter Two examples, had its year-end on 31st December.

Sounds obvious, so far – but nothing in tax is obvious. Companies House, to whom you have to submit statutory accounts, assumes your year end is the end of the month in which you register. The Revenue, however, assumes you start trading on the day you register, and time all its dealings with you from that date – so, for example, if Futura had actually started trading on 12th December 1993, the Revenue would time its expectations of when it expects documents from you from that date.

This may seem trivial, but companies can get into hot water for submitting information 'late' because of confusion about year-ends.

The Revenue has its own year-end, rather bizarrely on 5th April – which shouldn't affect your business, but which many readers will have come across via their personal tax returns (for an explanation of this date, see the box!) This is called the tax year or 'fiscal' year.

You can change your year-end for Companies House to a date that suits you: contact them and they will send a form.

Why the 5th April?

We've long wondered why this date was chosen, and have recently found out.

In medieval times, the beginning of the year for legal purposes was 25th March, Lady Day, the Feast of the Annunciation. This was logically the true 'beginning' of Christianity, Christ's conception, exactly nine months before Christmas; though the choice of date is also probably a throwback to an earlier, pagan mythology, when the New Year was celebrated on that day because of the spring equinox. (And because nature is beginning to get its act together around then: 25th March is arguably a much better New Year's Day than 1st January: our gardens, and medieval peasants' fields, are pretty quiet throughout January, February and early March...).

The start of the legal year moved to 6th April because of the reform of the calendar. The earth doesn't go round the sun in exactly 365 days, but in just over 365¼ (365.256363 to be precise), hence the need for complex calendars with leap years. The original calendar, which dated back to Julius Caesar, assumed exactly 365¼, and was getting out of sync with reality. On the continent, the calendar was reformed in 1582 by Pope Gregory XIII, whose Gregorian ▶▶

calendar cut out the leap years at the turn of three out of four centuries. Traditionally sceptical about Euro-initiatives, we Brits kept the Julian calendar for another 170 years, but finally had to step into line and adjust our calendar to Gregory's system. The old 25th March suddenly became 6th April. One result of this was the change of the start of the legal and accounting year to the latter date. Another was massive rioting, with people demanding 'give us back our 11 days'!

Beermat.biz

VAT

Fear of VAT sends many small businesses scurrying into the arms of accountancy firms. It should not. Keep your Analysed Cashbook properly; pay the VAT on time; get a proper finance cornerstone as soon as you can.

In essence, VAT rules are very simple. You charge VAT on your goods and services (usually at 17.5 per cent); when the invoice is raised, you put that 17.5 per cent surcharge into a special VAT account. When you get charged VAT by a supplier, you can pay that surcharge from the VAT account. If your business is profitable, you will end up with a surplus in the VAT account that you have to send off to the VAT collector every quarter.

So VAT isn't just a sudden 17.5 per cent charge on your business, but a 17.5 per cent tax on 'what you charge your customers, less what you pay your suppliers'. That's still unwelcome, of course, but *c'est la vie*. 'In this world, nothing can be said to be certain, except death and taxes,' as Benjamin Franklin wrote in a gloomy moment.

You can register for VAT whenever you like, as long as you can show you are serious about trading. You should register if you are planning a large capital purchase. You must register once your annual turnover reaches £64,000, or will do so in the next 30 days. You register by filling in a form called, appropriately, VAT1, which you can apply for from HMRC (or fill in online). Get it via www.hmrc.gov.uk (click on 'VAT' and then on 'forms'). This is a useful website with all sorts of information.

Alternatively, call an orderline, 0845 300 6555.

You will be given a VAT number, and must quote this on all invoices.

VAT collection takes place quarterly. HMRC will send you a form, which you must send back – plus a cheque if necessary – within a month after the end of your VAT quarter. So if you register for VAT on 1st February, your first quarter will end on 30th April, and you will need to pay your first lot of VAT, for business done 1st Feb to 30th April, by 31st May. (Don't worry too much about these dates – HMRC will let you know when they expect their money.)

The consequence of this is that you are effectively collecting tax for the government. Look on the bright side: if you sell an item for £100 on 1st February, you'll actually charge £100 + VAT = £117.50. When you get that amount in, £100 is yours, and £17.50 is owed to the VATman, but not until 31st May. So in a way the government is lending you money.

Just don't forget the government will want that money on 31st May, and will get very nasty if it doesn't get it. Put all VAT payments in a special account. Touch this money if you have to, but plan cashflow around the fact that such-and-such amount is going out to the VATman at the end of your VAT quarter – no negotiation.

You will probably get a phone call from HMRC after your first quarterly payment. Follow our advice and don't panic. Have your records to hand. If you have a finance cornerstone, let him or her do the talking. There may be some anomalies: still don't panic, as these are usually petty and easy to sort. This early contact is more about ensuring you're filling the forms correctly than checking if you are deliberately cheating.

You may also get a visit from HMRC. This doesn't mean much: be polite and open with the VAT inspector, and you shouldn't have any trouble, apart from a small extra bill for some detail you overlooked.

As with banks, if you feel you are getting out of your depth with VAT matters, contact the VAT people and explain, before they come and find out. Like all government departments it has a complaints procedure, a helpline (open 8am till 8pm, Monday to Friday: call 0845 010 9000), and the website. There is even a Debt Management Unit if you are foolish enough to spend all the money in the VAT account then have nothing left when the quarterly payment is due.

Of course, this will not be necessary with a proper finance cornerstone.

Some other points about VAT…

The various rates of VAT look more fearsome than they are: don't be spooked by this. Most businesses pay 17.5 per cent.

A piece of useful jargon: the VAT that you have to charge your customers is called 'output' VAT – VAT on the output of your business. The VAT you get charged by your suppliers – i.e. VAT on the inputs you use to make things in your business – is called 'input' VAT.

For a business selling direct to the consumer, the real hassle of VAT is the one-off price-hike of 17.5 per cent when you register. For any 'business to business' enterprise, this is not a problem: for your customers this will just be 'input VAT', which they can claim back against the VAT they collect from their customers.

Finally, note that there are a range of schemes whereby newly-registered and still-small companies can make the payment of (and accounting for) VAT even easier.

★ *The Flat Rate Scheme.* Companies with a turnover of up to £150,000 p.a. can pay VAT at a flat rate based on their turnover. The rate varies according to your business sector (and the likelihood that, as someone in that sector, you will make large capital purchases). For service businesses, the rate is around 10 or 12 per cent (there's a list that goes into specifics, 'Notice 733' from HMRC); for manufacturers around 8 per cent and retailers between 7 and 2 per cent. We recommend signing up to this very useful scheme, as it saves much accounting hassle.

★ *The Annual Accounting Scheme.* Companies with a turnover of less than £1,350,000 p.a. can pay nine instalments to HMRC, plus a balancing amount at the end of the year. This makes financial planning much easier.

★ *The Cash Accounting Scheme.* Big companies are liable for VAT the moment the invoice is raised. For companies with a turnover of less than £1,350,000, you do not have to account for the output tax on your sales until you actually get paid. Businesses can remain in the scheme until their annual turnover of taxable supplies reaches £1,600,00 and provided they have a good compliance record. We also recommend signing up to this: of all the VAT schemes for small business, this is the one that is most used.

★ There are *special schemes for retailers*, who have the biggest problem with the varying VAT rates and with the sheer number of transactions. Call the 0845 010 9000 helpline for specific details.

You have to register for these schemes. The VATman won't just put you on them because you qualify.

Of course, these schemes change over time. The best way to stay abreast of changes is via the VAT Notes which come with the quarterly return that HMRC send you. They may not be a thrill a page, but should be read conscientiously. The finance corner-stone should also read the professional press, especially the trade journal, *Accountancy*.

Corporation tax

Even as a seedling business, you are liable for corporation tax. Sounds grand, but our guess is, like most entrepreneurs, you'd forgo the grandness for the money.

You have to work out your tax liability yourself, then send the money to the Revenue – you can now submit online – along with your annual corporation tax return, form CT600, which you can get from HMRC online. Rather bizarrely, the Revenue wants the money nine months after your year-end (the Revenue's version of your year-end) but are happy to wait a year for the CT600 form: in practice everyone sends the money and the CT600 off together then gets on with something more interesting.

Until your turnover gets above £10 million (or if you lose more than £10 million, or if you have a capital gain of more than £10 million), the CT600 is a pretty simple document. Basically you send them a P and L account for the year, calculated according to certain rules. These rules cover:

★ *Capital allowances.* This is essentially about what you're allowed to depreciate and how fast. Cars, office furniture and plant and machinery can only be depreciated at 25% (using the reducing balance method), though a First Year Allowance of 50% can be claimed on office furniture, plant and machinery and computer equipment. Note that the allowance on cars is retsricted to a maximum of £3,000 annually.

★ *Allowable expenses* – i.e. ones that you can deduct from your taxable profit. The magic test is that the expense be incurred 'wholly and exclusively for business purposes'. In reality, this test is not watertight, and arbitrary lines have to be drawn. Travelling to your registered place of work is not allowable, but one-off travel is allowable (as are regular commutes as long as you are on a temporary assignment). If you work from home, a proportion of your heating, lighting, phone and insurance bills are allowable, but your mortgage is not. Protective clothing is allowable; your ordinary business suit is not (even if you're never seen in a suit outside the office). Accountancy and legal fees are allowable, unless your lawyers are challenging the Inland Revenue!

Note that you have to include any 'capital gain' made from selling an asset at a profit in the P and L you send the taxman (unlike for individuals, where income and capital gains are treated as separate sources of money). The longer you have held the asset, the less tax you have to pay: talk to a tax expert for the specifics.

This P and L will yield a figure for 'profit chargeable to corporation tax'. This is charged at the following rates.

On your first £300,000 of profits, you will be taxed at 21% as from 1 April 2008.

There is then a band of 'marginal relief', for companies making between £300,000 and £1,500,000 per annum. The way the revenue presents this is that it's a 'relief', something wonderful they are doing for you, a bit like sending you a nice Christmas present or helping you with some particularly onerous task. In practice, it is not a 'relief' at all, but a higher rate of tax you pay the moment your annual profits pass £300,000. The rate begins to inch up after that point, so you won't notice it immediately you cross the £300,000 barrier. But by the time your business is making £900,000 p.a., its tax rate will have crept up to 24.5%.

This full rate, which your business will be paying at and beyond £1,500,000 annual profit, is 28%. (That's £420,000 of your hard-earned £1.5m.) Fortunately the rate doesn't go any higher than that.

Sadly, a tax-free band of £10,000 – a nice idea to help small businesses get off the ground – was abolished because too many people were being smart and splitting their businesses into lots of mini-businesses each earning around £9,999. Such is the world of tax and tax avoidance, a perpetual 'arms race' between the revenue and tax experts.

Note the difference between tax avoidance, which is legal, and tax evasion, which is illegal. The former is recommended, unless the schemes are so complex that they gum up the efficient running of the business. As we've already said, the latter is to be avoided.

If you want to know how much tax you will be paying, the HMRC site has a tax rate calculator. Find it on

http://www.hmrc.gov.uk/calcs/mrr.htm

If, as an entrepreneur, you find this section has put your head in a spin, don't worry. Einstein said that it was 'the hardest thing in the world to understand', so you're in good company. Just make sure you get the right advice on this topic from your finance cornerstone.

For finance cornerstones, yes, of course the above is an over-simplification: remember that the place to get information on the minutiae of corporation tax is the profession. Just as you should have a favourite firm of lawyers, you should have a preferred supplier of arcane tax (and other financial) information.

PAYE and NI

Entrepreneurs have learned to live with VAT and corporation tax, but hate PAYE and NI. PAYE and NI are more complex, with different tax codes and tax tables for each employee. They have to be paid more regularly. They are more sneaky – 'employer's NI' is just another tax on business: why not call it that and be done with it?

Both of these only arise when you employ people: small wonder businesses prefer to hire in consultants wherever possible.

Note that even if you own the business, if you are a director and you take any money out, you are an employee for PAYE and NI purposes.

PAYE. 'Pay as you earn', or rather 'Your employer pays as you earn' (YEPAYE sounds far too upbeat an acronym for this chore), is how the Revenue collects Income Tax from employees.

When you take on an employee, they will have a P45 form from their previous employer. This divides into three: you keep a bit, the employee keeps a bit, and you send a third bit off to the Revenue. The P45 will have a 'tax code' on it, which tells you – via a set of tables which the Revenue will provide – how much money to take off the employee's monthly or weekly pay and send to the Revenue. (Note: employees for whom this is a first job, or who have been self-employed for a while, won't have a P45. Get form P46 from the Revenue, and treat as above.)

National Insurance (NI). Once upon a time this went into a special fund to pay for pensions and the NHS, but this stopped happening long ago. Both you and your employees pay, you at 12.8%, your people at 11% up to a ceiling, then 1%.

As we've said, 'employer NI' – the bit that comes out of your pocket – is simply a tax on businesses employing people. The government spends a lot of time saying how much it wants small business to create jobs, then slaps a tax on us when we do. (Oh, well, back to Ben Franklin again…) The most important thing to remember is that when you budget for taking people on, you must take this into account. If you are going to employ a bought ledger clerk for £15,000 p.a., you must budget for the NI you will have to pay over and above this (an extra £15,000 × 12.8% = £1,920).

You account for and pay PAYE and NI in the same way as VAT, putting the money into a special account every month (or every week for waged staff), then sending it to the Revenue at regular intervals. If the total amount of PAYE and NI you send each month is less than £1,500, then you can send it quarterly, but otherwise it has to be done on the 19th of the following month (or the 22nd if paying electronically). For example, Jayne earns £1,200 in May: she gets her salary on the 31st, less the amount due to the Revenue for Income Tax and employee NI. This amount sits in a special account till June 22nd when it's paid by BACS to the Revenue. You pay the relevant amount of employer's NI at the same time.

At the end of the 'fiscal' year – not your business year – you have to give a P60 form to each employee showing how much you paid them in the year and how much tax was deducted. You also have to send two forms to the Revenue summarising payments, P14 and P60. These have to reach HMRC by 19th May. By 9th July, you have to send two more forms to HMRC and to each employee, P9D and P11D, and a P11D(b) to the Revenue only. Note that if you use form P11DX to get a P11D dispensation, you don't have to put quite so much into the two P11D forms.

If this makes you want to:

★ Become an anarchist

★ Give up enterprise and go back to a nice safe job with Megacorp

★ Emigrate

we understand. But better to:

★ Make sure your system is computerised. Even basic accounting software handles most of this stuff with ease

★ Get a professional to do the work created by the tax system. Not the finance cornerstone: they have better things to do (but if you have a finance cornerstone, he or she should be responsible for delegating this work, either to an experienced bookkeeper or an outside agency)

★ Get on with building the business.

Other hassles

Student loan repayments. If you take on a graduate, they'll probably have to repay loans – which they do via PAYE. The Revenue will send you a 'start notice' if this is necessary.

Stakeholder pensions. The government wants as many people as possible to have second pensions, to prop up the ailing state pension scheme. Currently, it wants people to get this second pension either via an occupational pension (which you tend to get if you work for a large organisation), or by a stakeholder pension. The latter is new and affects small businesses: you, the employer, have to at least offer to set this up and run it for your people, selecting the provider from a list of big names and paying a small piece of their wages/salary into it. If any employee wants to participate, you must run the scheme for them.

The scheme kicks in early: once you employ five or more people (this figure includes yourselves, entrepreneur and cornerstones, even if you haven't paid yourself any money yet!), you must offer this service and 'designate a stakeholder pension provider'.

In theory, you can be fined up to £50,000 for not offering a stakeholder pension scheme once you pass this threshold: in practice, OPRA (the pensions regulator) isn't out to persecute start-ups – but set a scheme up anyway.

How? With whom? Get expert advice: later on we talk about getting an HR consultant on your side. They should be able to help you sort this out.

Uniform business rate. The corporate version of council tax: you pay your local authority an amount based on the rateable value of your premises. It's called 'uniform' because the 'multiplier' (the amount by which your rateable value is multiplied to work out how much you owe) is set nationally rather than by each local authority. Not because the rate is uniformly unpopular with small businesses up and down the country – although it is.

If you rent a serviced office, you won't see this (though, of course, it will be a factor in your charges). Otherwise, if you own or rent offices, you will be liable for this.

If this part of the book has filled you with gloom, don't let it. Yes, this tax stuff is a pain, both in time and money. But hundreds of thousands of businesses up and down the land deal with it. Modern computer software helps hugely, as does an experienced bookkeeper (more on this most valuable asset later). Even HMRC do their bit to make it less fearsome. There's plenty of help around.

The law

This is not a handbook on company law – if it were, even more trees would have to be cut down and there would be more hernias in the book distribution industry. But we do need to touch on those aspects of law that have particular effects on the finance of start-ups and small businesses.

Just as we advised entrepreneurs to get a finance cornerstone as soon as possible, we advise anyone with a small business to have legal advice on tap. Not from an insider, as it's a tap you run a lot less frequently than finance, but from a local firm of solicitors. Get networking if you don't know any! Finance cornerstones reading this section should make it their business to have 'pet' lawyers, whom they can always go to when problems arise.

There are four main areas we need to discuss. One has already been covered, that of company registration (we put it in the seedling chapter because we felt it belonged there). The others are Intellectual Property, insolvency/wrongful trading and the various stages of liquidation. We trust that if you follow the advice given in this book, you won't need to use your knowledge of the last two topics, but they need to be understood.

Intellectual Property

We're not going to go into this in much depth, but a few comments are in order.

Some businesses will have as a differentiator some special piece of intellectual property (IP) or branding. Someone needs to be thinking about protecting this, and the best individual to be that someone is the methodical, cost-conscious finance cornerstone. In a technology company, look at selective patenting: the finance cornerstone and the innovator should find a patent agent who will talk you through the process, and, more important, give advice on when to patent and when not to (entrepreneurs and innovators often waste money overprotecting their IP). For service companies, the best protection from copycats is delighted customers, plus a solicitor's letter to anyone guilty of outrageous plagiarism. The best team member to interact with lawyers is the finance cornerstone.

Insolvency and wrongful trading

In essence, a company is *insolvent* if it can't pay its debts. The technical description is a lot more complex than that, but that's what it amounts to.

Wrongful trading is if you place orders with suppliers when you know, or ought to know, that you are already, or you are about to become, insolvent. Note the wide-ranging nature of this definition. Ignorance of your company's financial position is no excuse (all the more reason for getting a finance cornerstone), nor is the fact that you weren't technically insolvent when you placed the order but were just about to become so.

If your company goes into liquidation (see below) and you are found to have been guilty of wrongful trading, the court can order you to 'make a contribution to the company assets' (a nice way of saying 'pay the company's creditors out of your own pocket'). What about 'limited liability'? It's invalid if wrongful trading is proven.

Badly-run businesses often slip into and out of technically being insolvent, delaying payments to creditors until other payments come in from debtors. It's only if the business goes bust that the notion of wrongful trading will kick in, so people can carry on this way for years. However, it's risky practice. Avoid it.

If you do find yourself drifting in and out of insolvency, treat it as a flashing red warning signal. Get your act together!

★ Stop saying 'the money will come from somewhere'. One day it won't.

★ Talk to an Insolvency Practitioner (IP – confusingly the same acronym as for intellectual property). People often leave this till too late, fearing that IPs love snooping round businesses then killing them off. Actually, IPs like helping and saving companies, just like vets like healing animals and only 'put them down' when all other avenues have been explored. Another fear is that 'IPs cost a lot of money'. They cost a heck of a lot less than they save you – and some will have an initial chat with you for nothing.

★ Don't order anything else, even if it is needed to make stuff you hope to sell.

★ Investigate potential investment

★ Redouble efforts to recover debts

★ As with any cash crisis, talk to creditors and try and negotiate a way out

Document all the steps you take, a powerful defence if a creditor does lose patience and you end up in court.

The route to liquidation

As we've said, chronic cash-flow problems are signs that a company really isn't cutting the mustard. If you follow the advice in this book, you should not end up that way – but supposing you are a finance cornerstone bought in to turn round a company like this, or are an entrepreneur who has for some reason (inheritance; ignoring our advice about takeovers) acquired a business in this state. You may find yourself sliding down a nasty slope into liquidation.

If you are not a specialist in corporate intensive care, get advice straight away from a licensed IP. He or she may be able to give you advice that will enable you to turn the company round without using any special procedures. Well done them. Otherwise... below we list the most common procedures. Readers in Scotland please note that the law is slightly different for you.

The first is a *Company Voluntary Arrangement (CVA)*. This is a way of staving off creditors without much court involvement. The company prepares a proposal to reorganise and turn around the business, using procedures such as disposal of assets, reduction (or delay in the payment) of liabilities, and refinancing. The proposal then has to be approved at a meeting of creditors and shareholders. The scheme is carried out under the supervision of a licensed IP.

Administration. The company usually obtains an administration order when insolvent (or likely to become so). The order protects the company, its business and its assets from the creditors. A licensed IP, here known as the *administrator*, is put in charge. His or her aim is to save the company, or to get more for its assets than a liquidation would realise. He or she will prepare detailed proposals to achieve these aims, for approval at a creditors' meeting.

Liquidation. If it is thought that there is no prospect of selling or rescuing even a part of the business, then an IP will normally recommend that the company be put into liquidation. Although the shareholders pass a resolution to do this, it's the creditors, who can appoint their own *liquidator*, who controls the process. This is called a Creditors' Voluntary Liquidation (CVL). If the directors/shareholders choose not to liquidate (or can't agree to), then one or more creditors can petition for the company to be wound up: the ultimate ignominy of a Compulsory Liquidation.

In either case (CVL or Compulsory Liquidation), this is the end of the line: the business will be wound up and the assets sold for whatever the liquidators can get, which is usually not very much, especially once costs have been deducted.

Dodgy business people can put their company into liquidation, then buy back the assets cheap and 'phoenix' the business, starting all over again with a clean slate and different partners. Creditors just get shafted. The law has been tightening up on this, but it can still happen.

Less dramatic is the *dissolution* of a company. The business is solvent, but has reached the end of its useful life. It needs to go through a formal winding-down process. Talk to an IP, who will probably recommend a Members' Voluntary Liquidation (MVL). The IP will realise any remaining assets, ensure all creditors are or have been paid off and distribute any remaining funds to shareholders. The MVL prevents people emerging from the woodwork years later, claiming you owe them money. Tough: a proper procedure has been followed and the company no longer exists.

Note that people often talk about companies going bankrupt. This is incorrect usage: people become bankrupt, companies are liquidated. Of course, a sole trader can go bankrupt – set yourself up as a limited company and you can avoid this.

You may also hear about a *receiver* being appointed, instead of an administrator or a liquidator. The main difference is that while administrators and liquidators act for all creditors, receivers act for a specific one (though they do have a 'duty of care' to other creditors). The rules have now changed, however, and receivers can only act in cases where the relevant debt was incurred before 15th September 2003.

But enough on this gloomy subject!

Chapter Five: Accounting 102: basic management information

In Chapter Two, we talked about certain basic essential tools of the trade, focusing attention on the balance sheet and the P and L, and the statutory format in which they have to be submitted to Companies House. This chapter deals with the main tools needed in the growing company to keep the team informed of what is going on in the business.

People who look at this material then say 'I'm an entrepreneur/salesperson/design genius (or whatever else); I don't need this stuff' are being prats. You are all business people, and this material is essential to doing business well.

Break-even point and 'contribution'

A simple question asked early on in the life of the company is 'when do we start making money?' The correct but infuriating answer is 'it depends what you mean by making money'. Clearly the first milestone is when the first piece of real money comes in

– a very real cause for celebration. But a more solid target is required, a point at which the business can be said to be 'washing its face'. That is the Break-even Point (BEP).

To establish this, a clear distinction needs to be made between fixed and variable costs.

Fixed costs are costs you can't change, however many – or few – items you sell. Examples include rent and rates on premises, long-term leases, wages/salaries of full-time staff, general administrative expenditures (e.g. of head office), fees to essential outsiders such as auditors, bank interest on long-term loans, and depreciation on fixed assets.

Yes, full-time staff and premises are not 'fixed' for ever, but to dismiss or move from them takes time and money. On a month-by-month basis, which is the time frame you need to use to establish your break-even point, they are effectively fixed.

In contrast, *variable costs* are all those costs that vary with the number of items you produce: cost of the raw materials, costs of anything (machines, premises) or of anyone hired just to do a particular job, costs of getting your product to the customer, costs of after-sales service – this last item can be considerable if a product turns out to be a turkey.

Note that the fixed/variable distinction is similar, but not the same as, the distinction between direct and indirect costs which we made in Chapter Two. Indirect and fixed costs have a lot in common, as do direct and variable costs. But direct costs include depreciation while variable costs do not; indirect costs include distribution which is largely a variable cost. So why do we need two sets of distinctions? The first one is essentially about rules to ensure that everyone's statutory accounts are comparable. The really useful distinction is between fixed and variable costs, and that is the one we will be focusing on from now on.

Get the notion of variable v fixed cost clear. Run through some examples in your mind. Got it? Good: it's very important.

Your break-even point occurs when you are getting in enough sales revenue to cover both the variable costs of making what you sell and the fixed costs incurred during the time frame you are looking at.

For example … you sell 1,000 items in July at £40 each, bringing in £40,000. The variable costs of those items amounted to £28,000, so your gross profit for the month is £12,000. Hurrah! But you have fixed costs to meet too. Let's say the fixed costs of the company are £18,000 per month. You're not making a real, net profit at all – despite all that busy-ness, you are still £6,000 worse off on 31st July than you were on 1st July.

The natural question is, 'Well how many of these damned things do I need to sell to start making a real profit?' Easy! Each £40 item covers its variable cost (£28 per item). The remaining £12 is best looked at as a *contribution to fixed costs*. Your monthly fixed costs are £18,000, so you need 18,000/12 = 1,500 contributions to pay for them. 1,500: that is your BEP. When you sell your 1,501st item (within the time period, of course), its £12 contribution will no longer be to fixed costs, which have been covered by the previous 1,500 sales, but a *contribution to net profit*. (It'll *be* the net profit if you only sell 1,501 that month.)

Break-even point can also be expressed as a £ sales figure. In the example above, the company needs to turn over (£1,500 × £40 =) £60,000 worth of business a month to break even.

The graph opposite is another way of explaining the concept.

Of course, life isn't as simple as this. You may not sell all you produce. You may sell lots, but customers start asking for bigger discounts as they buy more. Fixed costs may have to rise to enable increased production … the BEP is only a rough guide. But it has

The break-even graph

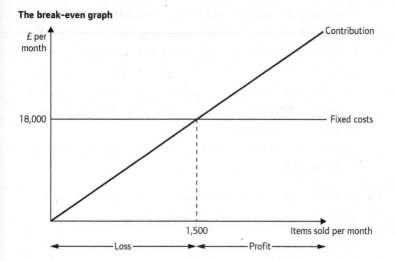

the virtue of being unambiguous and of huge emotional power. 'We're making money!' It is a metric that everyone in the business can use and understand, from the postboy to the entrepreneur. The fact that it is ultimately an approximation is a small price to pay for its power.

The same concepts and graph can be used to answer other questions. Some examples:

★ *'How many items do we need to sell to have a monthly net profit of £6,000?'* The answer is:

$$\frac{\text{Monthly fixed costs} + \text{desired profit}}{\text{Contribution per unit}}$$

which here is $\dfrac{£18,000 + £6,000}{£12} = 2,000$ units

(this could also be expressed as monthly sales of £80,000).

★ *'How many more items will we have to sell to break even, if we lower our prices by 10 per cent?'* (Beermat hint – don't lower your prices, improve your service!)

The new price of £36 will reduce the contribution to fixed costs to £8 per unit. This will mean you have to sell 18,000/8 = 2,250 units per month. In other words, 750 extra units – or *half as many again*. Hence the undesirability of price wars. Anyone who still thinks dropping your prices 10 per cent means you have to sell 10 per cent more stuff, please work through the calculation above again – and again and again and again until you understand its implications and they keep you awake at night!

★ *'Can we afford to offer a special discount to this customer this month?'*

The answer should depend on whether you have passed BEP or not. If you've already sold your 1,500 units this month, at their usual cost, you can afford to entice a new customer with a special, one-off (make this clear!) discount. Yes, we've said we're against discounts – if your product/service solves real 'pain', people will be happy to pay the full price for it. But if you must discount, only do it when you have passed your BEP and as part of a very specific plan to interest a specific, potentially long-term customer.

★ *'Supposing we raise our prices by 10 per cent?'*

The new price of £44 will increase the contribution to fixed costs of each sale to £16 per unit. So you'll have to sell 18,000/16 = 1,125 units per month. That's 375 fewer, or 25% less. So get thinking – how can we justify that price rise; how can we send the customer away smiling and thinking 'we paid extra, but, boy, was it worth it!'?

★ *'How many more items will we have to sell if we spend another 10 per cent on fixed costs?'*

Here the answer is 10 per cent. New monthly fixed cost (in our example) = £19,800, which divided by the contribution per unit (12) is 1,650, 10 per cent more units.

★ *'Supposing our production process gets 10 per cent more expensive?'*

The new variable cost per unit in our example will be £30.80, leaving a contribution to fixed costs of £9.20 per unit. So the BEP will now be £18,000/9.2 = approx 1,950 – an increase of 30 per cent.

On modern spreadsheets, you can play around with examples like this forever. It's instructive to spend a bit of time doing so, so that the message of what causes have what magnitude of effect becomes instinctive. Readers for whom the examples above long ago became instinctive will, we're sure, forgive us for labouring the various points raised, as they are so important. For the rest of you, here they are in a box, to make sure they become instinct.

The Break-even box

In our fictional (but realistic) model:

Cutting prices by 10%	*means*	having to sell 50% more items to break even
Raising prices by 10%	*means*	having to sell 25% fewer items to break even
Raising fixed costs by 10%	*means*	having to sell 10% more items to break even
Raising variable costs by 10%	*means*	having to sell 30% more items to break even

---

Note that raising fixed costs looks a 'better deal' than raising variable costs. In the short term that is true, but the price you pay is loss of flexibility. In our view, this is too high a price: remember the maxim 'stay flexible' and avoid fixed costs wherever you can.

Keeping fixed costs down also keeps you out of the following trap, which is easiest understood using the notions of break-even and contribution. Businesses with high fixed costs will often do unprofitable work. Why? Because the very worst thing for them (apart from some kind of calamity) is for the fixed assets to be idle. As long as variable costs can be covered and a bit of contribution to fixed costs earned as well, such companies will want to do the work.

Imagine such a business, with fixed costs of £3,000 per month, which usually makes 100 items a month at a variable cost of £4 each. Usually they sell their goods at £40 each. So each sale contributes £36 to fixed costs/profits (and so they earn £3,600 contribution in an average month, covering the fixed costs and making a profit of £600). Then times turn bad, and suddenly their order book is empty. Someone comes along and says they'll order 50 items, but are only prepared to pay £10 each for them.

'That's a quarter of our usual price!' exclaims the entrepreneur, shooing the person away.

The finance cornerstone talks to the entrepreneur, who sheepishly gets on the phone and agrees the deal. Why? Because even at that paltry level, the deal is covering variable cost (£4 per item) and making some contribution to fixed cost (£6 per item). If they do no other business that month, the company has at least contributed £6 × 50 = £300 to fixed costs: pretty grim, but better than nothing.

Of course, such a practice is not sustainable, but it happens.

Cash flow projections

In the seedling phase, the most important thing for the business was for it to gain a foothold in the marketplace, for the idea to make the transition to a business. To make the next transition, to a *successful* business, the most important factor is cash.

Cash is the main cause of sapling company failure: the business runs out of cash, and the bank or exasperated creditors put it into administration. That the business is theoretically profitable is of no concern to them.

Profitable but cash-poor

This scenario, 'We're making a profit on paper but don't have any actual money', often puzzles non-financial people. How can this be? The answer lies in inverting all the advice we have given on cash control.

Remember that sales go into the P and L account, and thus count as 'profit', the moment they are invoiced. If the invoices don't get chased (or do get chased but not paid), you have theoretical profit but no actual cash.

Cheques sitting around the office are just pieces of paper until they reach the bank.

If you buy a machine for cash up front, you spend cash then. You will probably depreciate it (put the cost through the P and L) over several years, making profits look higher than cash levels.

If your P and L makes you think you've got more money than you have, and you go and spend that money; then a whole lot of bills come in that you suddenly have no money to pay; then the bank won't lend any more because they never see any cashflow forecasts from you ... that's how businesses go bust.

⌂ Beermat.biz

This message is not new. Back in 1494, Fra Luca Bartolomeo de Pacioli wrote: 'Three things are necessary to one who wishes diligently to carry on business. Of these, the most important is cash.' (The other two were a sharp-witted accountant and good financial information.)

Cash management begins with cashflow forecasting, and this begins with the sales forecast. The finance cornerstone should be talking to the sales cornerstone several times a week, and the centrepiece of the conversation should be the sales forecast.

In Appendix B we show a model sales pipeline.

Opposite is a model cashflow forecast.

This is a 'rolling' forecast because it is updated regularly – every month at least, preferably every fortnight. The updates should be thorough, too. Every figure should be looked at as if the forecast were being prepared for the first time, not just copied from the last forecast. You cannot take chances with your business's lifeblood.

Note the conservative sales figures for October and November. Many start-up sales pipelines look like this, but entrepreneurs and sales cornerstones shrug that off. 'Sales have always come in,' they say. The finance cornerstone has to be constructively pessimistic. Don't turn into Marvin the Paranoid Android and say 'no they won't': do point out that you need to plan ahead *in case* they don't.

In reality, Futura probably turns 'interested prospects' into 'actual orders' about two months ahead. Fine. Start worrying when the sales figures six weeks ahead look bad. (See Chapter Six for more on this essential topic.)

Note that VAT is collected as the customer pays (row 3), but only sent to the VAT authorities – minus, of course, all the VAT incurred in row 18 – quarterly (row 19). Futura treat this as cash

Futura Gadgets Ltd
CASHFLOW FORECAST (£'000)
for the four months ending 31st November 2007

		Aug-07	Sep-07	Oct-07	Nov-07
1	Cash in:				
2	From customers	106.0	109.0	65.0	57.0
3	VAT on sales to customers (17.5%)	18.6	19.1	11.4	10.0
4	From shareholders				
5	From a loan				
6	Total cash into the business	124.6	128.1	76.4	67.0
7	Cash out – cost of sales:				
8	Raw materials	(21.8)	(13.0)	(12.5)	(9.9)
9	Human resource	(31.4)	(24.8)	(23.6)	(21.8)
10	Other cost of sales	(12.5)	(9.9)	(9.4)	(8.7)
11	Cash out – overheads:				
12	Human resource	(18.0)	(18.0)	(18.0)	(20.5)
13	Marketing	(3.0)	(3.0)	(4.0)	(12.0)
14	Premises	(1.7)	(21.4)	(1.7)	(1.7)
15	Other expenses	(6.0)	(5.0)	(7.0)	(8.0)
16	Finance expense – interest payments	(0.9)	(1.1)	(0.9)	(0.9)
17	Capital expenditure (on fixed assets)			(23.0)	
18	VAT on expenditure (17.5%)	(7.6)	(5.4)	(9.8)	(6.8)
19	Settlement of VAT liability	(21.8)			(26.2)
20	Corporation tax		(15.0)		
21	Loan repayment	(2.1)	(2.1)	(2.1)	(2.1)
22	Dividend paid				
23	Total cash out of the business	(126.8)	(118.7)	(112.0)	(118.5)
24	Net cash in/(out) of the business [6+23]	(2.2)	9.4	(35.6)	(51.5)
25	Opening cash position	(9.0)	(11.2)	(1.8)	(37.4)
26	Closing cash position [24+26]	(11.2)	(1.8)	(37.4)	(88.9)
27	*Overdraft facility*	*(20.0)*	*(20.0)*	*(20.0)*	*(20.0)*

in and cash out like any other. The rule is to plan ahead for the quarterly VAT outflows.

The company no doubt also pays PAYE and NI, but these are subsumed in row 9 (human resource).

Note the 'lump' in row 14: though their balance sheet tells us they own some property, they obviously rent as well, and this is, as is standard, due on quarter days (March 25th, June 24th, Sept 29th, Dec 25th).

The small blip in row 16 represents a fee for the DTI Small Firms Loan Guarantee, which we will discuss later.

Note the corporation tax payable (row 20) on 30th Sept – nine months after the end of Futura's last business year.

Futura's finance cornerstone will be looking carefully at the sales figures to ensure cash is available to cover October's asset purchase and November's marketing campaign.

If you ask non-accountants to name the key sources of financial information, most will either say a bank statement or the balance sheet/P and L required by statute. In our view, none of these touch the rolling cashflow forecast. If you are an entrepreneur in a sapling business, and you want one piece of information from your finance cornerstone, ask for this.

Monthly P and L

However, good management accounts will also contain a backward-looking element, analysing the previous month's trading via a profit and loss account. As with all accounts, comparing them month by month is a particularly useful exercise, revealing welcome or unwelcome trends. Watch particularly for falling turnover and rising variable costs.

Opposite is a model set of monthly management accounts.

Futura Gadgets Ltd
MANAGEMENT ACCOUNTS (£'000) for the month ending 31st July 2007

		Actual	Forecast	Better/ (Worse) Than Forecast		Person Responsible
1	Sales (turnover):					
2	Volume sold (units)	1,800	2,500	(700)	−28%	Fred
3	Average price (£ per unit)	£55	£50	£5	+10%	Fred
4	Sales value [=2x3]	99.0	125.0	(26.0)	−21%	
5	Variable costs:					
6	Raw materials	(16.8)	(23.5)	6.7	+29%	Bill
7	Sub-contract personnel	(30.7)	(36.0)	5.3	+15%	Ann (Julie)
8	Other variable costs	(12.9)	(14.1)	1.2	+9%	Bill
9	**Contribution to fixed costs & profit [=4+6+7+8]**	**38.6**	**51.4**	**(12.8)**	−25%	
10	*Contribution as a % of sales*	*39.0%*	*41.1%*	*−2.1%*		
11	Fixed costs:					
12	Human resources	(18.0)	(18.0)	—		Ann (Julie)
13	Premises	(8.4)	(8.4)	—		Ann
14	Depreciation of fixed assets	(10.8)	(10.8)	—		Ann
15	Finance costs (interest)	(0.9)	(0.9)	—		Ann
16	Other fixed costs	(8.9)	(8.9)	—		Ann
17	**Profit/(loss) [=9+12+13+14+15+16]**	**(8.4)**	**4.4**	**(12.8)**	−291%	
18	*Profit/(loss) as a % of sales*	*−8.5%*	*3.5%*	*−12.0%*		
19	Stock days	75 days	40 days	(35 days)		Bill
20	Debtor days	55 days	40 days	(15 days)		Fred
21	Creditor days	55 days	60 days	5 days		Ann

Note the 'person responsible' column at the end. In this business, Fred is the sales cornerstone: note that he also is listed as responsible for chasing debtors – his customers, with whom he should have a good relationship (more on this later). Bill is the delivery cornerstone, Ann is the finance cornerstone and Julie is an outside HR consultant, for whose work Ann is responsible within the business.

Note also the mention of

★ stock levels

★ debtors

★ creditors

These items normally appear on the balance sheet. You don't need a 'monthly balance sheet', but these three key numbers do have to be updated monthly and to appear on the management accounts. They are best expressed as 'days' – effectively how long it takes a piece of metal arriving at the factory gate to turn into a sold product; how long it takes your debtors to pay up; how long you are delaying making your payments to your creditors.

Stock and creditor days are calculated by dividing the relevant figures by a daily average Cost of Goods Sold. If your annual Cost of Goods Sold is £100,000, your daily average is (obviously) £100,000/365 = £274; if you hold stock worth £20,000, you are turning that stock over once every 20,000/274 = 73 days.

Debtor days are calculated by a similar method, but using turnover rather than Cost of Goods Sold.

Futura's high figure for stock days is not good news for the company. The guess we made when looking at the balance sheet, that stock is piling up, seems to be right (row 19). Sales are way behind forecast, and debtors are taking longer to pay up than expected. The sales cornerstone is underperforming...

Once the business begins to produce more than one product category, management accounts must reflect this, breaking down income and variable costs according to product category. It's amazing how many businesses don't do this, and are subsidising a turkey with a range of good products without being aware of the fact. (It's fine to subsidise turkeys, as long as you choose to – for example if the loss-maker gives the business incredible prestige, and brings customers flocking in who then buy lots of other things.)

Monthly management accounts on a Beermat

★ Cash flow forecast

★ Profit and loss account

★ Key ratios

Stock days

Debtor days

Creditor days

Gross margin (= contribution to fixed costs)

Fixed costs as proportion of turnover (watch the sequence)

Sales/profit per employee (for service companies)

Beermat.biz

Chapter Six: # The Sapling Business: the idea really becomes a business

'We've got a business!'

That was a real cause for celebration.

It's also time to draw up a serious business plan, and to talk funding with the bank *if you need to* (remember, you may not need to: can you fund from revenue?). Many other changes will follow – and are the subject of this chapter.

If you have a finance cornerstone, they will start spending more time on the business. If you do not have such a person in your team, this lack is going to start hurting. Reread Chapter Two and find one! From now on, we are writing on the assumption that you have such a person on board.

The Real Business Plan

It is now worth spending time planning how you're really going to grow the business. It is the entrepreneur's job to put in the main strategic 'shape'. However, the finance cornerstone must play three key roles.

One is, obviously, the specific financial section.

The second is the 'numbers' in each section of the plan. We've seen far too many business plans that consist of a kind of expanded version of the company brochure plus some spreadsheets stapled to the end. There is no sense of connection between the two: the entrepreneur has drawn up the plan then asked an accountant 'can you do some numbers for this?' By contrast, a good business plan is suffused with financial sense. It is clear that the finance cornerstone has looked into all aspects of the plan and considered the financial implications. Relevant figures are quoted throughout the plan, not just in a kind of pointy-head's ghetto at the end.

The third role is to be a coach to the entrepreneur. Most entrepreneurs enjoy the early stages of drawing up the plan but aren't very keen on detail and/or may suddenly decide to change things. The finance cornerstone coach needs to keep them focused on the task, asking the difficult questions that a bank manager or angel would ask, and seeing the plan through to its end – a piece of work that is thorough, consistent and realistic.

Once the plan is finished, the finance cornerstone must *keep on* coaching, ensuring that the entrepreneur knows the plan backwards and can discuss it in depth with outsiders.

A good analogy is with ghost-writing, where the celeb is telling their story but the actual legwork is done by a professional writer. At the end, the celeb must stand up with a big grin and say

Memo to the finance cornerstone.

If the entrepreneur hates planning...

Your first job will probably be to insist the plan be drawn up. Book an hour of the entrepreneur's time, sit down with them and run through the template, noting their answers. On the basis of this, draw up a 'first draft' plan. This should then be fed back to them, to check it is really what they had in mind. When a draft is agreed, insist on it being circulated to the rest of the team.

A meeting should then be held, where everyone speaks their mind. Take proper minutes. Any disagreements that arise need to be ironed out: the best person to do that is the entrepreneur, but the wise finance cornerstone keeps an eye on things to make sure the ironing-out happens.

The entrepreneur should write the final plan – though if they really can't stick plan-writing, the finance cornerstone should write it and present it to the entrepreneur for approval. If the entrepreneur does not approve, then more ironing-out is needed.

⌂Beermat.biz

proudly 'This is my story!' not 'This is a book about me written by someone else'. In the same way, the entrepreneur must own the plan, but the finance cornerstone will have been the organising force behind it. This should be no problem to the finance cornerstone, who is not in business for glory but for decent money and the pleasure of doing an important job really well.

The whole plan should not be more than 20 pages long. We receive loads of business plans the size of phone books: to us this shows lack of focus. And if the idea is so great, why aren't you out there now, doing it, rather than writing vast tomes on the subject?

Rather than go into exhaustive detail about the plan, we've produced a simple template and put it in the back of this book (Appendix C). Feel free to use it: if you need something more complicated, there are loads of them available on the internet.

Some points on this template:

★ *The executive summary.* Keep this to one page. For readers external to the company, this will be the most important section. They will use it to get a feel of the business: 'I like the sound of this; let's read on' as opposed to 'Hmm – doesn't sound my sort of thing – still, I suppose I'd better read a bit more' or, worst of all, 'I'm not reading any more of this rubbish'. It's a bit like the jacket of a book, where the right blurb and design can make a huge difference to sales.

   When writing this summary, resist the urge to copy chunks of the main plan – rephrase everything; that way you won't bore the reader. 'Bullet' key points.

★ *The commercial context.* This is classic entrepreneur territory, but the finance cornerstone, especially if he or she has sector experience, will have useful input.

★ *People and culture.* After the executive summary, this is probably the most important part of your plan. Be thorough. The
outside reader will be particularly interested in the top team:
resist the temptation to embellish!

★ *The sales plan.* The finance cornerstone should liaise with the
sales cornerstone to get sales forecasts – but remember they
will always be estimates. You can be pretty specific when discussing costs, and even market size, but the figures in the sales
section will still contain guesswork and optimism, even
though you now have real sales under your belt.

★ *The financial plan.* Note the *sensitivity analysis*, which shows
how the main predictions will vary under certain scenarios.

Many people think that getting funding is what business plans are
for. This is never totally the case, and often not the case at all.
Their main job is simply to be a plan for the business to follow.
A road map to success. We know this sounds a trifle obvious, but
many businesses don't plan, and encounter huge problems. 'Failing to plan is planning to fail' does sound a bit like something
nanny says, but sadly it's true.

The plan, like the business model, also makes sure all the team
members are heading in the same direction. Looked at from this
perspective, writing the plan is as important as the finished art-
icle, which will be a kind of statement of an agreed purpose that
the whole team has been working towards during the writing.

Writing the business plan often winkles out unexpressed, unreal-
istic expectations, usually, but not always, in the mind of the
entrepreneur. Remember that a business plan should be realistic
but never lose its underlying tone of optimism. After all, you *are*
going to succeed.

Finally, yes, of course the plan can be used to raise funding. What
sort of funding? We discuss this later.

Cornerstone roles

The idea is now well and truly a business: legally, but more importantly in itself, in its culture and style. It has customers, and expects to get many more. It is taking up the time of able, busy individuals, and will soon start actually employing people. It is beginning to create wealth. Its needs are becoming more complex.

The finance cornerstone has an increasing role to play in all this, as custodian of the wealth created and as participant in the actual creative process. Both matter hugely. A number of themes emerge, which will now be dominant through the life of the business:

★ management information

★ decision support

★ cash

★ cost

★ administration

★ systems

★ strategy

★ funding

Let's look at these, one by one…

Management information

The first and most basic thing that the entrepreneur and the team will require from a finance cornerstone is proper information on the financial condition of the business. This should be provided via a fortnightly rolling cashflow forecast and monthly management accounts – both of which were described in the last chapter.

If the business is in trouble, the cashflow forecast may need to be more regular. We have seen ailing businesses where it was done daily.

Decision support

As well as the above ongoing provision of information, the finance cornerstone will be needed to assist with making larger, specific decisions. Entrepreneurs (and other team members) will often come up with 'Supposing we…' ideas. Customers may suddenly come up with requests: 'the five stores where we trialled your snacks said the customers loved them; we want to put them in 100 stores next month!' The finance cornerstone must work through the implications of these proposed changes – especially for cash flow. Effectively they draw up a mini-business plan for the new idea (a two-page discussion document is the ideal format).

Even if the ideas sound totally wacky, the finance cornerstone should be straight-faced and methodical in assessing them. Will importing some rather nice soup the entrepreneur had on holiday in France be the right thing for Smith Office Cleaners to do? Probably not, but a proper 'why not' case needs to be made.

The finance cornerstone must, of course, question every capital investment. What value does it bring to the business – does it improve quality, speed, reliability? Put a cash figure on that value. Yes, it might be a bit of a guess, but a good guess is better than no cash figure at all. Once this has been agreed, then the investment can be monitored. It will have its own break-even point: if it saves £1,000 a month on maintenance costs and costs £24,000, it should start paying for itself in two years. Is this a sensible figure? Will it last that long? Will it become obsolete before then?

Don't bother with more arcane calculations about 'weighted average cost of capital', 'net present value', 'internal rates of return' and so on. The above, simple, 'payback' method of analysis does the job fine (arguably better) and is readily understandable by the rest of the team.

The finance cornerstone should also look at ways of hiring or leasing the asset, to keep in line with our core maxim, 'stay flexible'.

In the classic Beermat company, every decision is a team one; in companies where the entrepreneur has the majority stake it is, of course, the entrepreneur's. In all cases, the input of the finance cornerstone must be studied with great seriousness.

Opportunity cost

This is a term that crops up a lot in decision support. Essentially it's about the question: 'what *else* could we do with the time/money?' If you have two options, A and B, and can't do both, the opportunity cost of doing A is the profit you would make from doing B. The notion needs to be used with care. In the wrong hands, it can become a brilliant tool for instigating total and perpetual 'paralysis by analysis' – logically there are always an infinite number of things one *could* do. Do not use this tool with indecisive people!

Luckily, entrepreneurs tend to be the opposite: action-oriented. The notion of opportunity cost is a neat way both of reminding them that alternatives do exist and of getting them to look at these alternatives.

Beermat.biz

Cash

The finance cornerstone as referee. There will almost undoubtedly be competing calls on the company's cash balances. A debt is outstanding, but the sales cornerstone doesn't want to upset the client by being pushy. The operations cornerstone has the opportunity to buy some stock cheap. The innovator has been working on this new process, and wants some money to test it…

The right person to arbitrate between these competing calls on cash is the finance cornerstone. Entrepreneurs, owners, team members and anyone who happens to be in the building at the time please note: if the finance cornerstone says 'we haven't got the cash', he or she isn't joking.

Cash crises. For sapling companies, a cash crisis often comes with their *first big sale*. Actually it's more than a cash crisis, it's a personal one: we've seen companies fall apart at this point. The entrepreneur and the sales cornerstone are delighted; the finance and delivery cornerstones are tearing their hair out. Extra people will be required, extra raw materials, extra space; all of these require cash – now!

What can be done?

If the finance cornerstone keeps in regular contact with the sales cornerstone – which, of course, should be standard practice – the new order will not appear out of the blue. So some 'what if…?' planning should have been done in advance.

The finance cornerstone will, as part of their 'decision support' function, check the details of the order to see if it is worth fulfilling. Can it be delivered profitably? Can it be delivered without the company running out of cash? If not, it must be declined. This may sound mad, but many businesses fail because of 'overtrading', taking on more business than they can handle and cracking under the strain.

The sales cornerstone should be asking for stage payments, including (of course) some payment up front. Don't forget that the new, quantum-leap-in-size order should have come from someone who really believes you can solve serious pain for them. In essence, they want to make you a 'supplier partner'. So what is needed is a payment system that suits *both* your needs. The sales cornerstone should negotiate one. You're a small business, and the fulfilment of the order will require expenditure on a level you're not used to. The buyer needs to be reminded of that. (Some big firms will simply reply, 'These are our terms, take them or leave them.' In which case, it's probably best to leave them. Small businesses can be destroyed by taking on excessively punitive orders.)

The danger of monopsony

This means 'having only one buyer for your output'. All textbooks warn against it, but people still fall into the trap because:

★ They're fed up with lots of tiny, high-maintenance clients

★ It looks glamorous to have a big name endorsing their product/service

★ The big, new client holds out the prospect of massive growth without any further sales effort – particularly alluring if the business has no sales cornerstone and nobody in the business really likes selling

▶▶

Get a sales cornerstone, and task them with building a balanced portfolio of clients. 'Balance' is about the proportion of your business you get from any given client: by all means have Megacorp as a client – but don't start relying on them to provide all your business.

If one buyer wants more and more – you've got a better product than you thought. Gear yourself up for fast growth, and get selling this amazing stuff to everyone else. If the one, eager buyer insists on exclusivity – how much is it worth? Why don't they buy you?

Beermat.biz

The finance cornerstone should make a careful plan for fulfilling the order, with all moves carefully costed and documented. It's like doing a new business plan. Then he or she should take this plan to the bank, and talk it through with them. Do not do this before the order is confirmed: as we've said, banks don't like surprises, but they don't like unnecessary panic either.

And, of course, remember the maxim 'stay flexible'. Don't buy fixed assets to fulfil the first big order, just in case it turns out to be a one-off. Hire them. It's amazing what you can hire (an entrepreneur we know hired a giant custard-making machine to fulfil one special order).

The issues above are going to crop up over and over again as the business grows, so get used to them. Handling them is a key finance cornerstone skill, like the cover drive for a batsman or the B$\flat$ scale for a musician. This is why we say finance cornerstones must be experienced: dealing with this stuff has become instinctive for them.

The opposite of the sudden big order can also strike – a *sudden collapse of orders*.

Again, action needs to be taken immediately. Pretending the problem will go away is never an option. The sales cornerstone needs to get things moving again, fast. At the same time, the finance cornerstone has to get working to ensure the company stays cash positive. Ways of doing the latter quickly are:

★ Cancelling any planned special expenditure (e.g. an asset, a planned team outing, a specific ad campaign)

★ Chasing debtors more vigorously

★ Talking to suppliers and asking for better payment terms

★ Talking to the bank and asking for an increased overdraft

If this kind of problem recurs, the team may need to take another course of action:

★ Get rid of the sales cornerstone and find a new one

In more detail:

Upcoming expenditures on assets. We assume the business is 'thinking cash', and really has to purchase the asset. If original plans were to fund that purchase from cash, fund it instead by a loan secured on the asset.

Chasing debtors. (We are assuming you already have a good system in place for doing this – see below if not.) Get the sales cornerstone to talk to his or her favourite customers and offer a discount for early payment.

Suppliers don't want you to go out of business, and may well be prepared to discuss payment terms, especially if they are told it is a one-off request. What can you offer in return?

If nobody is prepared to negotiate, then you will just have to delay payments. The team should discuss and decide which ones. Some points:

★ If you are faced with a mountain of invoices from the same company, at least pay some of them, so they know that you're not completely broke

★ If you can, pay key suppliers first, then small companies who need the cash flow. This isn't just being nice: you don't want a small supplier going bust

If none of the above yield enough cash savings, it's time to *talk to the bank*. Remember that talking to the bank is essentially the finance cornerstone's job, not the entrepreneur's.

Many small business owners (and finance cornerstones) spend their time lurching from one of the above scenarios to the other, then back again – the famous 'feast or famine' problem. There's no magic way out of this, but the following thoughts might be of consolation:

★ Good sales forecasting can mitigate this problem

★ Good finance cornerstones become used to dealing with both scenarios

★ Almost every other small business has the same problem

Most of all, feasts and famines will be best dealt with by companies that set up the right financial institutions and mindset early on. It's often in the sapling stage that those early cultural fixes begin to pay big dividends.

Cost

For the seedling, our advice was to avoid expenditure wherever possible. Now you have a business, we can change that to '*spend sensibly*'.

Sometimes expenditure is necessary, in which case go and spend it. Fly budget rather than full-fare, but don't stay at the cheapest hotel in town when you get there, if it means you go to the next day's meetings red-eyed, half-asleep and vaguely nauseous from a fat-laden 'full English breakfast'. We know a small computer repair business who refused to kit the staff out in uniforms on cost grounds; we persuaded them to get uniforms, and the repairers looked so much smarter that the business was able to raise its rates by 30%.

Remember the maxim 'stay flexible': hiring may be more expensive than buying in the long term, but the flexibility that it buys you is another piece of sensible spending.

When acquiring the use of assets:

★ only get what you need: basic kit that does the job, not stuff with fancy features

★ make sure it is in good condition

★ make sure the terms are flexible

★ pay as little as possible, consistent with the points above

Asterisk point two above is a reminder that given the choice of a) borrowing a rather ropey old machine off a mate, which you're not sure will deliver to the quality you require, or b) hiring a decent machine – go for the latter.

Ultimately, all spending decisions are about *value*, not just money. Rising costs that create even greater value should be good news.

Make sure it is real value that is being created, however. A lot of 'profile building' is money down the drain – the classic recent example being boo.com, which became very famous for a while, sold virtually nothing and ended up losing around £80 million. When accused of profligacy, the company replied that staff 'only flew Concorde when they had to'.

Remember that great brands are not created by expensive advertising, but by customer delight over time. The odd piece of awareness-building is fine, especially for a retail/entertainment business, but don't throw too much cash at it.

Beware of *creeping costs*. You need a warehouse for a short while. You end up renting one on a longer lease than you need, as that's all that's available. As you now have the warehouse, you start storing stuff there. When the lease finally expires, you renew it, as nobody has time to go through what's there and decide if you really need it or not...

Steve joined a club a while ago, with the express intention of getting some business from the chairman. FDUK did some work with him, then the chairman left the area. Steve's still a club member, renewing by direct debit every year, though he hasn't been there for more than a year.

Company credit cards can lead to creeping costs: reserve them for the founding team only, and make it clearly understood that the finance cornerstone can question any expenses on them.

Another form of creeping cost is creeping product overcomplication. Entrepreneurs and sales cornerstones are always on the lookout for opportunities, and like to jump in to meet them. This is fine, but it can lead to an entrepreneurial business having too many product lines, or spending too much effort customising its products. Customisation is a good thing in so far as it keeps customers happy and creates entry barriers around what you do

– but it can become prohibitively costly. The finance corner-stone needs to keep an eye on this.

One trick for keeping costs under control is to 'move accountability down'. Ask the people who actually do the work if they really need a new x to do their job – they may well say no. Also, more junior people tend to be poorer, and thus less used to thinking about spending large sums.

Systems

This is a classic area where money needs to be spent – wisely, of course. The sapling business needs to develop its systems: the old, informal ones that worked fine at the seedling stage will soon become potential disasters.

Most important of all is a new *accounting system*. Don't be talked into buying an expensive one 'because it gives you plenty of room to expand'. Buy a cheap software package, use it to its full potential and then, when the company is much bigger and richer, upgrade several levels.

Sage is the market leader. Accountants love it, as it has lots of accountant-friendly features. Entrepreneurs often prefer Quick-Books, as it's easier for laypeople to understand. Either system will do fine. QuickBooks comes in a number of versions: the cheapest one is around £130, and will do basic tasks including payroll. For around £400, you can get a more complex system that will last a long while. If you are planning to grow to any size, then this is the system we recommend. Sole traders will do fine with the basic £130 system.

Whatever you buy, the main cost is not money but *time*, as everyone in the business has to get used to working with it.

The best way to understand modern accounting software is to understand the old systems that it has replaced.

Back in the old days, accounts were kept in ledgers, actual books where transactions were noted down by clerks with names like Bob Cratchit or Lupin Pooter. The key ledgers were the purchase and sales ledgers, which featured invoices received or sent. These ledgers were usually broken down into sections for each major account holder, so it could be seen how much business had been done with each one in any given time frame.

When money actually came in or went out, it was entered in the 'cash book', a ledger that listed all transactions where money actually changed hands. (The cash book is not to be confused with the *petty* cash book: the bookkeeper will have a tin on their desk with a float of cash to pay for sudden, minor requirements like the boss having forgotten his sandwiches – the petty cash book keeps a record of what goes in and out of this.)

As well as these, a special 'register of fixed assets' was kept. Remember that purchases (and sales) of large, fixed assets don't feature in the Profit and Loss account.

There was a 'journal' to enter odd items such as depreciation or to rectify errors.

You may come across the term 'suspense accounts'. These are created by bookkeepers when the books don't balance, 'suspended' till the problem gets sorted (or left hanging there, if nobody had the skill or courage to sort this). You also get a great deal of suspense from wondering what the account hides – possibly some minor oversight, possibly all kinds of mismanagement. If you find a set of accounts full of these, be cautious.

The whole accounting process was controlled via a master ledger called the nominal ledger. This essentially contains summaries of all the other ledgers, called 'control accounts'.

At regular intervals – banks do this every day, global trading banks every eight hours, small businesses need only do this every month (but can do so on modern software at the click of an icon)

– the nominal ledger was checked in a process called Trial Balance. If the books balanced, everyone was happy; if they didn't, Tiny Tim didn't get his Christmas goose.

An accountant assessing a new set of accounts will probably do a quick trial balance, a bank reconciliation (see below) and take a look at 'aged debtors', which is not a group of old men who've hit hard times but a list of who owes money to the company, sorted by the length of time the debts have been outstanding.

Note that your software will not use the old terms: it will ask you to 'input supplier invoice' rather than 'open purchase ledger'; it will do the necessary 'doubling' entries automatically. But we think it helps to understand how things used to work.

A business that sells to the public will also need a system *for accepting payment* by credit and debit cards. Ask the bank, who will provide the system and lease you the machine(s) – at a price. The price is a commission on each trade. Negotiate on this: they ask for 4 per cent, which seems excessive to us. We know people who have got their rate down to 2½ per cent by insisting on a 2 per cent rate then finally conceding the half.

If you are trading online, set up a PayPal account.

More informally, you will need *systematic ways of doing basic things* like raising invoices, chasing debtors and making purchases. The finance cornerstone should make these standard practice.

Raising invoices. If you deliver physically, bring the invoice with you. Get the client to check both the goods and the invoice, and to confirm that both are in order. They are? Ask the client to sign a delivery note to that effect. Then leave them with the invoice. Couriers, if you use them, will tell you when the goods have arrived and have been signed for – invoice then. On long-term contracts, specify certain days on which milestone payments will be invoiced and when payment will be expected.

A useful hint from Mike: get the sales cornerstone to deliver some of your invoices by hand. They should phone first – 'I'm passing your way, shall I drop in the invoice…?' When they get there, they ask to see their contact, and have a brief chat: a nice excuse for a bit of account 'farming'.

Chasing debtors. Correct handling of this thorny issue begins even before an order is placed:

★ Once a new prospect looks reasonably likely to turn into a sale, ask around to see if they are good payers or not. People know, and are often prepared to say. Yet another example of the value of networking.

★ It is standard practice for someone on the finance side (either the cornerstone or the bookkeeper) to ask a potential new customer for *trade references*, and for the customer to suggest sources of them. Nobody need be offended by this process. If the customer appears offended, they are probably either new to business, in which case they have to learn this is standard practice, or an old hand who is also a poor payer.

★ *Bank references* tend to be of little value.

★ *Credit Reference Agencies* will charge, and often have out-of-date information. Avoid them: there is no short cut to getting proper trade references.

★ If someone turns out to have a bad reputation, tread carefully if you desperately need their business, and avoid them if you don't. It really isn't worth the hassle. If you must deal, ask for payment in advance.

★ Make sure your *terms and conditions* (see below) are clearly stated and accepted before any deal is done. This should be the job of the sales cornerstone, who in turn should be discussing upcoming deals with the rest of the team. The finance cornerstone's job is to ensure the salesperson is asking for and getting acceptable terms: sales people are often overkeen to get business, and can skip these 'technicalities'.

★ You are, of course, *sending your invoices* out as soon as possible… Have a system for this (see below).

★ You should send out monthly statements to all customers. These can be prepared on computer.

Once payment is missed:

★ A polite phone call from the bookkeeper is the first action. If relevant, check that the item has actually been delivered, and simply remind the customer that payment is now due. This will probably produce an answer along the lines of 'We'll get a cheque off as soon as possible.' Ask when their next cheque run is.

★ A second call, to the same person on the day after the cheque run, just to check that they did run the cheque after all. You may get the reply: 'Oh, good heavens, we forgot!' Stay cool; keep playing the game (for that's what this is). 'Never mind. You will get it in the post today, though, won't you?'

★ If, after a week the cheque has still to appear, a third call could play the good cop/bad cop game. 'My FD's on my back. Can you help me out…'

★ After this, the finance cornerstone should call the head of finance of the errant company.

★ If these initial attempts by the finance people to get payment fail, refer the matter to the *sales cornerstone*. In the Beermat business, the sales cornerstone (or, later, one of his or her team) has a personal relationship with the client. Time for them to talk the issue through (and to insist on action!). The sales cornerstone must also stop doing any selling to that company

★ The *entrepreneur* could talk to the boss of the non-paying company.

★ If these fail, it's time to formally *get tough*. No more supplies till the last lot is paid for. The sales cornerstone may well panic at this point – 'We're losing a customer!' – but their objections *must* be overridden. (The entrepreneur may well support the sales cornerstone here: the finance cornerstone just has to be firm. A reminder that a non-paying customer isn't really a customer might help.)

★ There are two threats you can make. One is to spread the news about the non-payment among the business community (a powerful threat from a well-networked entrepreneur). The other is the law. The latter is expensive, diversionary, slow and probably less frightening than gossip. However a solicitor's letter can work wonders: worth it for any debt over about £250.

★ If the solicitor's letter fails, many creditors give up, as court action takes up so much money and time. But if you never put your threats into action, word will get round. So follow up *some* solicitors letters with court action and bailiffs.

★ When you do give up, the debt is formally a 'bad' one and has to be accounted for. Take it off debtors in the balance sheet, and put the loss through the P and L (where it was formerly recorded as income). Let your network know this company has let you down; not for revenge, nice as that might feel, but because you get information out of the network and should put information into it, too.

Note: some businesses simply take the law into their own hands and turn up at errant clients' premises asking for the goods back. Clearly this only works for certain goods. If you do this, don't threaten violence, and if you are threatened, don't get into a fight. If you have retained 'right of title' in your terms and conditions, the property is still legally yours, but you don't have the right either to force your way on to premises or to use force to get it back.

We mentioned *terms and conditions*. In theory your customers should always read these and consent to them: in practice they get skim-read at best. Never mind, you still need them. There are plenty of 'Ts and Cs' in the public domain: you can buy them off the internet, and we even know businesses who copied competitors' (!). Wherever you source them, you should have your solicitors look them over, to ensure they are up to date and appropriate.

Note the point about right of title above: part of the 'Ts and Cs' should say that goods remain your property until paid for.

Ts and Cs should also be part of any service contract. You can print them on the back of invoices or, if you trade online, invite people to view them.

Finally, the business will need a proper *Purchase Order* (PO) system. Make it cover as many purchases as possible – even utilities are no longer a routine purchase.

If Jones wants to buy something, say a hatstand for reception, he fills in a PO. The bookkeeper (see below) will have these standard forms, numbered sequentially; let's say the hatstand order is PO 134. Jones then takes PO 134 to the relevant superior, who 'OKs' the purchase by signing the order. Jones then goes ahead and orders the item, then returns the PO to the bookkeeper, who puts it in a special 'Open PO' file. When the invoice from Amalgamated Hatstands comes in, the bookkeeper matches PO 134 to it. When the item arrives, it is checked against the PO and the invoice. If all match, the invoice is marked as payable. When it falls due, a cheque is drawn and the finance cornerstone signs it.

Taking on a bookkeeper

It is not the finance cornerstone's job to keep the books, but to interpret them. The sapling business needs a bookkeeper.

We have seen businesses where the bookkeeper is probably the most important person in the company. Such a person is usually a middle-aged lady, and is the person to whom everyone in the business – including the entrepreneur – goes when they are upset. She spends a lot of time negotiating internal disputes. She also keeps the entrepreneur's diary (something entrepreneurs are often incapable of doing), acts as office manager, and even appears at key meetings with cups of tea at the right moment. If you want proof of her complete indispensability, visit the business while she is on holiday, and see the ill-natured shambles it quickly turns into. In leadership theory such a person is called the 'psychological leader', and quite right too. In ordinary life, a common term is 'mother hen' – a term that some readers may find patronising, but we find that people to whom it applies use it with pride.

If you can't get one of these marvellous people, get the next best thing. Someone with experience and character. The best way to find such a person is to ask around. If this doesn't work, place a small ad in the local paper. You will get a range of replies, but it is easy to spot the applicants with the 'right stuff': usually one or two stand out, and a brief interview is all that's required.

Agencies will find you bookkeepers, but at a price. We are not convinced they add sufficient value to justify this premium.

Some bookkeepers may wish to work part-time: useful to start with, but you will probably miss out on the 'psychological leadership' that way. If your part-timer is very part-time, don't wait for him or her to prepare and send invoices – do it yourself, at once.

The bookkeeper will have a range of duties, along with the obvious one of recording all transactions:

★ *Raising invoices.*

★ *Chasing unpaid invoices.* The best bookkeepers have a mixture of firmness and tact, the former ensuring that unpaid invoices get pursued relentlessly, the latter that the business relationship remains undamaged in the process. Lesser bookkeepers don't do this: if you hire a bookkeeper who is excellent at most areas but too mild to chase debtors, the finance cornerstone must do this job.

★ Preparing and sending out *monthly statements* to customers.

★ *Paying supplier invoices.* As we've said, best done weekly or fortnightly, in a bill-paying session where the bookkeeper matches due invoices to purchase orders, writes the cheques and gets the finance cornerstone to sign them off.

★ *Daily taking cheques to the bank.* Yes, electronic payments should be encouraged wherever possible but there are many 'late adopters' out there, so the ritual daily bank visit will continue for a while.

★ *Payroll, PAYE, National Insurance.* Modern accounting systems make these uncomplicated, though still a chore. A good bookkeeper should be able to handle these, but, if they can't, the finance cornerstone should have a relationship with an HR consultancy who will do this for you.

★ *Bank reconciliation.* Every month the bookkeeper should go through the bank statement and check that everything in the cash book is reflected in the bank statement and vice versa. Have cheques gone missing? Has the bank made mistakes? The 'bank rec' is not just a useful check on your dealings with the bank, but one of the few ways you can easily get a perspective on your own accounting system and its accuracy.

★ *Office supplies*. The best bookkeepers will look after these basics, ensuring the stationery cupboard is properly stocked.

Administration

The bookkeeper will do some admin work, but the burden of this will fall to the finance cornerstone. Not that they have to *do* all the admin, but they are responsible for it getting done. As the old adage has it: 'the buck stops here'.

Arguably, admin is 'all the other stuff not done by the other cornerstones'. It includes:

★ *HR*. This is the biggest headache, and we have thus dedicated a separate section to it below.

★ *Relationship with lawyers and tax specialists*. The finance cornerstone is the right person to deal with these people, because he or she will have a mindset similar to theirs, and because he or she is most aware of costs – which these professionals can rack up surprisingly quickly. As we've already said, the best finance cornerstones have 'pet' lawyers and other specialists who they can reach by just picking up the phone.

★ *Insurance*. Another of the finance cornerstone's pet experts should be an insurance broker specialising in corporate work. They should have a good relationship so that the broker only sells the insurance that the business needs, probably via some kind of package.

Once you have an office, you should have *contents* insurance. When you start employing people (other than directors), the law insists you take out *employer's liability* insurance, protecting you against employee claims for accidental injury, death or disease arising out of their employment. In practice, manufacturers should also seek some kind of *product liability* insurance, and service companies simple *professional indemnity* insurance. Retailers should look at *public liability* insurance (for injury to third parties, or damage to their property, caused 'during your business activity', which effectively means while on your premises).

Other types of insurance include:

★ Business interruption – covers lost revenue for a specified period, as well as debtors outstanding when the interruption started.

★ Directors' and officers' insurance.

★ 'Key man' insurance (we assume this covers key women too…)

All these are handy, but they all cost money

★ *Basic office admin.* Supplies, security, cleaning, phones. Give the bookkeeper as much say as possible in these, but always remember that the finance cornerstone is ultimately responsible.

★ *IT.* Yet another area where the finance cornerstone needs to have a pet consultant they know, like and trust. Pros can sort this stuff out quickly and well. Many entrepreneurs love meddling in this: a waste of everyone's time and effort!

★ *Property maintenance.* This should not be the ultimate problem of anyone in the business – you're leasing office space, remember. But even so, someone has to keep a check on things, complaining to the landlord if problems arise and chasing them to sort the problems out. As with other basic admin, a good bookkeeper will be up for this. But the responsibility ultimately lies with the finance cornerstone.

★ *Health and safety.* A potential minefield, and much best left to the HR consultant we are about to introduce.

★ *Archiving old documents*. The Revenue insist you keep 'all supporting documentation' going back six years. Err on the side of caution here, ignoring impulses to have a 'big tidy-out' – HMRC can get nasty even if you've genuinely lost something but they think you're pretending.

In the old days that meant box files lining the walls of the office. Now it can just mean CDs or memory sticks. It must not mean 'it's all on computer' – which could crash or be stolen.

Shred all documents, like drafts of finished work, that you don't need to keep.

Note that some people, especially overworked finance cornerstones, argue that the operations cornerstone should be in charge of the above tasks. Sadly, they are wrong. The financier's natural eye for cost efficiency and order is what is required. The operations cornerstone is a technical expert, master of their area but not of general office procedure.

The best finance cornerstones actually embrace the admin challenge, and go further. They become experts on what everybody in the company does. They spend time in each department seeing what people do, asking them about their job – which aspects they find difficult, which aspects of their environment help them and which hinder. This can make them a lot of allies – people like being listened to – and gives them a real picture not only of what the business does but how it gets done.

This is particularly useful for anyone coming into an existing business as a new finance cornerstone. They should forget the macho rhetoric about 'hitting the ground running' and take a little time to find out the exact shape of that ground. Even if a business is hurtling towards the rocks, time taken to talk to disparate people in the organisation is time very well spent. Remember that most problems in business boil down to people.

Taking on the 'Dream Team'

Big companies have huge HR departments. Who's in charge of this job in the start-up? Guess...

However, the finance cornerstone cannot be expected to be an expert. HR is getting ever more complex, as more and more rules kick in for smaller and smaller companies. How many people do there need to be in a company before you have to appoint a First Aid officer? What are the laws about disabled access to premises? You need professional advice on HR issues.

Getting such advice can be a problem, as most HR consultancies are big businesses serving other big businesses. However, this is changing as enterprising HR consultants, often sole traders or small partnerships, spot this gap in the market. The whole team should use their networking skills to find the latter kind of consultant. Talk to your local Business Link.

Once the right HR consultant is found, the finance cornerstone should be in charge of liaison with them. Issues to be covered should include:

★ *Director Service Agreements*. The HR consultant will draft these

★ *Formal letters* offering jobs. They will have a template

★ *Contracts of employment*

★ *Company Handbook*. They will have a template

★ What to do if you have to *dismiss somebody*

Outsiders should not run your recruitment; they should oversee it, ensuring that it is done correctly. You must do your own recruiting: no job is more important than filling the concentric circles of 'founding' team (entrepreneur and four cornerstones) and 'dream team' (next fifteen or so employees). Advertising for these should be a last resort: existing team members should look through their own networks first, for people they know, like and trust.

The relevant cornerstone must conduct the interview, with the entrepreneur watching and chiming in with questions from time to time. Follow your gut feeling if someone looks good on paper but 'feels' wrong.

For the 'dream team', the people that fill up the sapling business, you need energetic, imaginative, cheerful, team-playing 'doers'. The world seems to divide into people who do stuff and people who find excellent reasons for not doing stuff: insist on the former.

If you select the right sort of people and make work fun for them, you will rarely have to dismiss anyone. If you are having trouble with an employee, talk to the HR consultant first, to ensure dismissal is correctly handled.

Another role of HR in big business is monitoring staff performance, usually via six-monthly assessments. These should be done by the relevant cornerstones, the specific directors to whom the team report. As usual, however, someone has to check the reviews are taking place and to archive the results, and as usual this job falls to the finance cornerstone, until a proper HR department is set up.

Strategy

You made the big strategic decisions when working out your original business model and then when you wrote the Real Business Plan. These should be adhered to, especially the vision (unless the market has radically shifted). However, it's easy to drift, especially if lured by short-term tactical opportunities (a particular problem in companies where the entrepreneur is a sales person). The metaphor of a plane is often used: it has a clear destination, but can easily be blown off course, in which case a correction needs to be made – to the course, not the destination!

The Plan needs to be revisited regularly, to ensure it is up to date. But at the same time, it should not be tinkered with unnecessarily. Probably the best way to avoid such tinkering is to have radicals and conservatives in the founding team argue it out: do we really need to make this change? Innovators, entrepreneurs and sales cornerstones tend to be radicals; operations and finance people conservatives.

If the market has totally changed (or was not well understood at the time of drawing up the Plan), then a new destination may need to be decided on. This is the kind of thing you read about in business books – how IBM changed from making tabulating machines to computers, and then, two generations later, to computer services. It all sounds very exciting, but can be hell in a sapling business. People have got used to one vision: change it, and morale will plummet.

There's no easy answer to the dilemmas posed by the above. As a general principle, the more tactical the planning, the easier it is to change. Those core parts such as the elevator pitch, that say what customer pain you are in the business of solving, should remain unchanged. The rise and fall of dotcoms is perhaps instructive. Companies that got carried away in dotcom mania failed: companies that went on doing what they did well, and used the web as an adjunct to, rather than a replacement for, their current services, prospered.

One strategic issue that may rear its head is partnering. Do you want to 'get into bed' with a larger company? There are all sorts of issues here for a book on strategy, not one on finance. On a purely financial level, the finance cornerstone should check out the financial status of any intended partner. Are they actually as healthy as they purport to be?

Funding

If you followed our advice, you should have started a good relationship with your bank. Keep it.

Despite our observation in the seedling section about not asking for money at once, remember that banks do like to lend money (just as people, after a few dates, often like to sleep together). They don't make much money out of clearing cheques or from savings accounts; they do make money by lending to good, solid businesses who pay them back on time. So your custom, now you can show you are a good, solid business, is of huge value to them.

When you do ask, have your Real Business Plan ready.

One thing that can go wrong is that the bank manager you liked suddenly leaves, to be replaced by someone to whom you take a dislike. You can try moving branch – but consider moving banks. It's easier than many people think, especially if you have been a good customer.

Everyone in the team should understand the two types of bank lending, and how they operate.

Overdrafts should be used to finance short-term financing requirements: working capital or to cover small head-office expenses. Their great benefit is flexibility: they are not a licence to go out and blow the money at once, though sadly some businesses treat them as such. If you are always near your overdraft limit, you are not getting the real benefit from it. The ideal overdraft is used only sporadically, as the account dips in and out of credit.

A sensible level of overdraft to ask for is the amount of cash you usually spend in a month (your monthly 'cash burn', to use the jargon).

The downside of overdrafts is twofold:

★ They can be called in at any time, without much explanation. Banks will argue that they only pull the rug from under companies that are about to fall over anyway, and that if you have a good financial cornerstone, who does things like manage finances prudently and inform the bank in advance of problems, this will not happen.

★ Overdrafts are more expensive, pound borrowed for pound borrowed, than loans.

Loans are for longer-term financial needs. They should be for fixed purposes, for example to buy a machine or to fund an expansion into a new market. They should be structured accordingly – if you are planning to use the machine for four years, the loan should be repayable over that period.

Such a loan will be 'secured' on the asset – in other words, if you default, they can come and take the asset away. Other loans will involve the bank taking a 'floating charge' on the company's general assets – if you default, they can come and take away anything they like. Avoid these if possible, except via the SFLG (Small Firms Loan Guarantee) scheme (see below).

Monthly loan repayments will be a mixture of interest and capital repayments, the latter ensuring that if a borrower goes totally broke halfway through the period of the loan, the bank will have got some of its money back.

In the long run, banks prefer loans to overdrafts. If you have been running a large overdraft for a while, the bank may seek to convert at least some of it into a loan – bad news if you are planning to expand and actually need a bigger overdraft to cover increased working capital requirements. A good finance cornerstone will prevent this happening, but we have been called in to help cornerstone-less companies who have had this unpleasant surprise sprung on them.

Take note of the excellent *Small Firms Loan Guarantee* scheme operated by the Small Business Service of the DTI. This guarantees loans for small firms with good business propositions but to whom the banks won't lend because the business owners have no security (or have had the sense to put their house in joint names with their partner, so the bank can't take it away). Guarantees are available for loans lasting from two to 10 years and of sums between £5,000 and £100,000 (£250,000 if you have been trading for more than two years) to companies with under £3m turnover (£5m for manufacturers).

What actually happens is that if the bank likes your business (or you) enough to want to lend to you, but finds out you have no security, it will put you forward to the SBS recommending you for a guarantee. Given the bank's recommendation, it is a formality. Once the paperwork is done – it should take about 15 minutes – the bank passes the form on to the DTI, which usually responds within three to four weeks. You are then covered (or covered enough to make the bank happy: the guarantee only covers 75% of the loan).

There is a small (and effectively negligible) fee to pay for the guarantee, based on a percentage of how much is covered, payable quarterly.

Finance cornerstones should be knowledgeable about the various *grants* available. As we've said, what grants are available from where is perpetually changing: there's no point in going into specifics here, talk to your local Business Link. A couple of days spent with one of their advisors will set you back a few hundred pounds, but could open the doors to healthy amounts of grant money.

Business Link – saviour or quango?

While we're on the subject of Business Link … the organisation, which is effectively a franchise of government services to small business, has not had wonderful publicity. But we have met some great people in Business Link, who are highly competent and really care about their clients. The sad truth is that the service offered by the Link is patchy – outstanding in some parts of the country, mediocre in others: the government is not a strict or savvy enough franchisor. All new businesses should check out their local Link, to see if it is a flyer or a flop. (Good entrepreneurs will network, and the word will get round about the local Link.) If it is a flyer, make full use of it – it's there to help.

Even if you get a bad feeling – failing Business Links are cliquey but at the same time over-eager to sell you consultancy – they still have an obligation to provide basic information on matters like grants, so use them for that.

And don't write off all institutionalised support for business if your local Link is poor. There are other bodies – Regional Development Authorities, Chambers of Commerce – where you might find a kindred (and knowledgeable) spirit.

⌐Beermat.biz

Grants tend to be for specific projects, such as a new product or training programme, rather than general corporate growing pains (which is often what you want finance for). They also rarely cover the entire cost of the project. But, if appropriately chosen, they are hugely helpful. So choose them appropriately, and use them.

Two major caveats. First, avoid – like the plague – grants that make you give away equity or which insist on controlling your decisions. We have come across grant-awarding bodies which insist that you buy services, goods and consultancy through them. This is at best high-handed and at worst corrupt. Avoid, avoid, avoid.

Secondly, beware of starting a project because someone, somewhere is handing out grant money for it. We know of businesses who have done this, and found that it has a) ruined their strategy and b), because the grant wasn't 100%, ended up creating expenditure. Yes, we know the old adage 'follow the money', but it's *customer* money you follow, not grant money. Grants are there to help you along your chosen strategic path.

A less serious caveat is the complaint by entrepreneurs that grant applications are bureaucratic and waste time. What is intractable bureaucracy to an entrepreneur is standard stuff to the finance cornerstone, who should manage all grant applications.

The Beermat approach to funding is to fund from simple sources. At the start: initial share capital from the team or friendly investors, revenue, grants, a bank overdraft for working capital, a bank loan for basic 'kit' if unavoidable.

Later you may need more. We talk about angel and VC (Venture Capitalist) funding in the next chapter.

Finally, don't forget that funding is only a means to an end, ensuring the company has the cash it needs when it needs it. The better you manage your cash, the less funding you will need.

Sapling funding

Requirement	Funded by
Working capital	Revenue
	Bank overdraft
Any fixed assets you have to buy	Do you really have to buy…?
…Yes, we must buy an x	Bank loan secured on asset
Other expenditure	Revenue
	Bank loan covered by SFLG
	Grant, if 'available, appropriate and unconditional'

Beermat.biz

Chapter Seven: The Young Tree Business: managing profitable growth

The business is now on the move. The decision has been made to move beyond the 20-person 'boutique' and to grow as quickly as possible. Culturally, there are all sorts of changes. The sapling organisation was tribal: everyone knew everyone else, well; everyone 'mucked in', doing what needed doing; the atmosphere was like a top sports team (hence our term for the people you take on in that phase, the 'dream team'). It was like The Three Musketeers: 'all for one and one for all'.

By contrast, the young tree is increasingly a place of specialists and of employees – the latter being solid and conscientious (you're not going to employ them, otherwise) rather than versatile, imaginative and passionate. Balanced against this loss (a loss many entrepreneurs feel intensely) is a greater stability. At the beginning of the journey, you could only say, 'we've got a great idea'. Now you can say, 'we've got a great business'. Growth will be fast, as more and more customers come to realise the value of what you do. During this phase, the future of an exit with serious money for the founding team (and decent payouts for everyone else who has made the success possible) becomes increasingly less of a fantasy (though not a reality till the next chapter...).

What new challenges are there for the finance cornerstone?

Management information

The tools we outlined in the previous chapter are robust enough to continue to serve you in this phase. You probably don't need fortnightly rolling cashflow forecasts: make them part of the monthly management accounts. The latter will also need to be expanded, breaking them down into product categories or markets.

Ratios get talked about more as the company grows, probably because they simplify something that is fast becoming complex. There are hordes of them – comparing every statistic about the business to every other statistic. Entrepreneurs are supposed to know about these (and finance cornerstones to be masters of them). Actually, we think most of them are vastly overrated.

Ratios are most used in the investment community, which stands outside businesses looking in – often trying to peer in through rather obscure windows like annual statutory accounts. Ratios help make these windows a little less obscure – but you are insiders, with much better information such as monthly management accounts at your disposal.

Nevertheless, some ratios are useful. We've already introduced the main ones:

★ Gross and net margin

★ Stock turnover

★ Debtor and creditor days

Other ratios only need to be looked at annually, to spot trends. These are:

Liquidity ratios. There are many versions of these, the best known being:

★ *Current ratio.* Current assets/current liabilities
        – for Futura, it is 455/205 = 2.22

★ *'Quick' ratio.* (Current assets – stock)/current liabilities
        – for Futura, it is (455 – 200)/205 = 1.23

These ratios are useful (they show Futura to be in good shape), but the management team have access to even more useful information. Rather than spend time calculating these ratios, the finance cornerstone should be getting on with the rolling cash-flow, which *really* tells you about liquidity. Outsiders don't have recourse to management accounts, and have to make do with second best, calculating ratios from published accounts.

Return on equity (RoE). This is calculated by dividing annual profit by shareholders' funds. In (classical economic) theory this is the touchstone for the company. Could the founders have done just as well leaving their money in a building society?

Entrepreneurs tend to pour scorn on RoE. They're in this business because they love it and because they are going to change the world. Or because they get all sorts of lifestyle benefits from the business, which don't show up in the RoE figure.

Asset turnover ratios. Asset turnover itself is reached by dividing turnover by (total assets less current liabilities) – for Futura this is 1,600/(785 – 205), which comes to 2.8. Again, this is only really interesting to an outsider. You should be looking at your assets – machinery for manufacturers, space for a retailer, people for a service business – and checking they are used efficiently. A chain of stores will find 'sales per square foot' an essential ratio. All well-run service businesses keep a very close eye on the proportion of chargeable time worked by each of its front-line people – especially the people at the top.

Gearing ratios look at various aspects of the debt/equity balance. We like the ratio:

$$\frac{\text{total assets less current liabilities}}{\text{shareholders'funds}}$$

but there are other ways of assessing gearing (such as, simply, all debt/all equity). Gearing is a measure of risk: the more indebted the company is, the less able it will be to ride out any storms.

But like the other ratios above, it is of much more use to investors than busy managers. Gearing ratios are supposed to answer investor questions:

★ 'Can this business pay its debts in the future?' You have a cash-flow forecast to answer this.

★ 'Can it afford to take on more debt?' Ask the bank! If all your assets are already secured against current loans and you have the full quota of SFLG, the answer is 'no', whatever your gearing ratio.

Larger businesses will have gearing ratios built into their 'covenants', the agreements they have with their banks – but such agreements are not common practice in the SME sector.

Ratios are of most use when wearing your outsider's hat and looking at other companies, either because you want to buy them (be careful!) or because you seek to emulate them. But for internal management, apart from the key ones we mentioned at the beginning of this section and the asset turnover ratios specific to your business, they aren't worth losing any sleep over.

Some thoughts on *budgets and forecasting...*

Budgets are the staple fare of large corporations, but we find them to be of little use to growing businesses. Things just change too fast!

Clearly, specific initiatives, such as an advertising campaign, need to be planned – a mini business plan, as we suggested in discussing decision support. An estimate of costs will form a part of this, which is in effect a budget. But this figure cannot be allowed the rigid power it has in the large organisation: what matters is to hit the tactical and strategic targets that made the task worth undertaking in the first place. If it goes a bit over budget, find the cash; if it costs less than you think it will, spend the cash elsewhere.

Of course, this is all in the context of our advice to spend sensibly. If a project is beginning to look like it will wildly overshoot the estimate in its mini business plan, then action needs to be taken.

Forecasting is also largely a big company thing. We question how much use it is even there – the world changes fast, and even Megacorp must move with those changes. But in the small business, grand forecasting is pretty pointless.

This does not, of course, mean that there is no view of where the company is going. Quite the opposite:

★ The entrepreneur should be keeping alive and ablaze the vision of the company as first expressed in the elevator pitch. Who are we? What is magical and special about us?

★ The finance cornerstone should have a clear understanding of the 'key drivers of financial performance' – how much we sell, at what kind of margin (gross and net), whether there are any big expenditures looming. Based on these, he or she can rustle up an approximate forecast pretty quickly. No one will take it as gospel, and no one should, not because the cornerstone doesn't know their stuff, but for the reason outlined above: things are changing too fast. You can't know where you're going to be in a year's time, and that's all part of the fun of being in a 'young tree' business.

★ Some 'what if…' scenario planning is a good idea.

Instead of forecasting, the team should revisit the Real Business Plan every year, to ensure the plan still reflects where the company wants to go and how it intends to get there, and whether reality chimes with this. As with drawing up the plan in the first place, this is important for lots of reasons, including the key one of getting the key people together to discuss and compare expectations and assumptions.

As part of this process, we recommend a Beermat Day, when the whole company goes somewhere off site and discusses the plan in an informal manner. Make sure the day is fun!

Decision support

Keep the system simple. Continue to resist the clamour to use all those fancy terms (WACC – weighted average cost of capital, NPV– net present value, etc.). Steve and Jeff both spent many hours at business school learning how to use these tools, and have found them of very little use in helping entrepreneurs build successful businesses.

What will change is the number and magnitude of potential decisions that the finance cornerstone has to examine. The company should now be generating cash. Rather than satisfying all those clamouring voices between which the finance cornerstone had to referee in the sapling section, this extra cash will simply make everyone clamour more loudly and ever more confidently in support of bigger and grander projects.

One particular area where we advise caution is takeovers. See the strategy section below for more detailed thoughts on this.

Cash

The uncertainty that made the 'first big sale' so scary should have gone: now you have a slightly different problem. Sales should be coming in with some regularity, but costs don't rise in a nice steady way to match (more on this in the next section). Sudden injections of cash become necessary.

Where do you get this cash from?

★ The bank should lend to you to purchase an asset.

★ Banks also have more sophisticated finance packages, allowing growing companies to borrow against things like inventory.

★ Start looking for outside finance – business angels.

★ Take another, hard look at the balance sheet.

We'll deal with the first three points in the section on funding. As regards the balance sheet...

If you are having problems with debtors, consider *factoring*. Factoring agencies will buy the debt off you at a discount and collect it themselves. Sounds great, but there are two downsides, which need to be dealt with.

The first is that you lose a channel of communication with your customers. You should be talking to your late payers yourself, not getting a third party involved. There may be other issues at stake – perhaps the late payer is dissatisfied with some aspect of your product and/or its delivery, but for some reason isn't telling you. Hence the role of the sales cornerstone in chasing debts.

The second is an image problem. The arrival of factors is often taken as a sign that a company is in trouble. If you do go down the factoring road, the sales cornerstone should arrange to have a chat with your main customers, explaining that you are still a robust business.

Invoice discounting is a more sophisticated form of factoring, whereby you do the chasing yourself, so retain the client contact, but there's a sophisticated financial arrangement whereby some of the burden of risk is taken away. Perfect! There is a catch: it's costly. It's also only used by companies with annual turnover of more than £1m. But if you are entering that league, need cash badly, and have recalcitrant debtors, this can be a way forward.

Cash can often be got from a balance sheet via fixed assets. No, you should not have acquired these if you've been following our advice, but entrepreneurs don't always listen to their finance cornerstones. Or you may be a finance cornerstone, newly bought into a sapling company which has been overspending money on assets for years. Now is the time to sort the balance sheet out.

Properties should be mortgaged – that way you keep the asset and its potential to increase in value.

Large, sturdy items that hold their value, such as a computer-controlled lathe/milling machine (but not more basic IT gear, which loses value fast), can be 'sold and leased back'. This is conceptually self-explanatory: you sell the asset to someone who then leases it back to you. Naturally, the details of any given deal are a lot more complex. If you must go down this route, talk to a specialist in this area (your finance cornerstone should know of one: if they don't, talk to your bank).

You read a lot about sale and leaseback in the financial press, because PLCs are forced to think short-term for various reasons (new CEOs eager to make a quick reputation; City analysts demanding quarterly growth etc.). This is a quick way of appearing to release 'shareholder value'. However, they are not a pure gain – you have a new regular, fixed cost (the lease), and you no longer own the item. For the private company they should be regarded as a necessary evil if you hit a cash crisis.

Cost

Costs, especially fixed costs, don't rise in a nice straight line. Instead, they do so in leaps, and in leaps of differing sizes. This is a particular problem in manufacturing. You acquire a machine (a big leap), and work it single shift for a bit. Orders grow, so you have to make another, smaller leap, to working double shift. Then three-shift, so the machine is now working 24/7. The market is still shouting at you to grow, and you believe it will carry on doing so (probably even louder as time goes on): you need a new machine, new premises for it, new people to work it. Even if you rent rather than buy, your fixed costs are about to take a great leap.

Graphically, we have a kind of staircase of ever-rising monthly fixed costs:

The fixed cost staircase

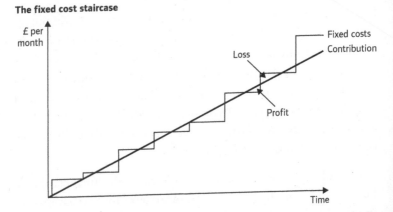

Rising 'through' this staircase is a line plotting contribution (to fixed costs/profit) per month. We have kept this line straight, which would be a dangerous assumption in the early life of the company. Now that the business has outgrown its sapling phase, this assumption is more likely to approximate to the truth of reasonably steady sales growth. (If anything, it's a little pessimistic: your growing reputation should mean the contribution line curves upwards.)

The contribution-per-month line cuts through the 'treads' of the staircase, at what are effectively new break-even points for each new version of the business. The areas where monthly costs exceed monthly contributions are, not surprisingly, areas where the company is losing money.

The staircase is, of course, uneven, like the steps you find on hill footpaths, some large, some shallow.

The Fixed Cost Staircase is a fact of business life, and not just for manufacturers. Any retailer seeking to create more space or open a new branch will hit a 'step'. Even service companies can encounter it: we know a small firm of accountants who took on a highly-paid tax specialist, then found they had much less work for her than they thought (remember that wages and salaries are as much a fixed cost as leases!).

What do you do about it?

Firstly, remember the maxim 'stay flexible' and consider if you really do need to raise fixed costs, or if you can add variable cost by outsourcing. This is particularly important if your need to expand is driven by a rise in sales you feel may not last. Get the extra items made in China or the extra software written in India.

If you feel the demand is permanent, or for other reasons outsourcing is not appropriate, then the whole team needs to discuss the implications of the next move up the Fixed Cost Staircase. As with any piece of decision support, the finance cornerstone needs to draw up a mini business plan for what will be in some ways at least, a 'new' business.

Admin

As the company grows, so must its finance department. In the sapling phase it probably had a bookkeeper (full-time, though she did many other things in the company) and a finance cornerstone, whose commitment to the business was growing. Naturally this commitment will grow even further as the business makes the great leap to a fast-growing 'young tree'. We reckon that by the time you have 100 employees in the business, the finance cornerstone will need to be full-time (though other finance cornerstones go full-time earlier, realising they are on a winner).

When the business makes its decision to leave the relative safety of the 20-person sapling and go for growth, the finance cornerstone will need to appoint a *financial controller*. This is a full-time job for someone who will:

★ build an accounts department. They may take over the bookkeeping at first, but will be looking to appoint clerks to run the various ledgers as the work expands.

★ take charge of systems, evaluating the software and thinking two years ahead: what kind of volume will we be handling then? The original £400 system should still be coping fine, but if the company grows to 100 people in two years it will start to creak and something newer and bigger will be needed.

★ The controller will also take over many of the tasks that fell to the finance cornerstone in the sapling phase, such as insurance, property maintenance and archiving.

The ideal financial controller is like the cornerstone, qualified and with specific experience in growing SMEs. The main difference between them is one of temperament: the controller is less happy with risk, more at home in a world of pure numbers, and not so interested in strategy. He or she knows they aren't going to set the world alight, but also that they are solid professionals without whom businesses would not grow.

As such, they are a clear and powerful symbol of what the business is becoming: it is 'growing up', taking on quieter, solid managerial types. There may be a bit of friction between the old guard and these incomers – a wise entrepreneur and cornerstones understand this, and make sure the new arrivals are supported.

What of the bookkeeper, whose pivotal role will be whittled away by the controller? There are various options. Some just leave, and join a new small company. Ambitious and bright bookkeepers may be studying and able to make the leap to financial controller, or (less of a leap, but still a career change) to running the nominal ledger in the growing business. Others may be happy to relinquish their financial role and concentrate on something they've been doing for ages, anyway – managing the office. Or the entrepreneur or the finance cornerstone may need a PA: male entrepreneurs will probably look around for glamorous young female PAs, but the bookkeeper would do the job many times better.

In the Beermat business, early team members are important, so the bookkeeper should be treated royally, especially if they were the mother hen and kept the whole place going in the early days.

The controller's first appointment will probably be a nominal ledger clerk, who may well do all the bookkeeping until sales, purchase, fixed asset register (in a manufacturing company), cash book and payroll clerks enter the department. These clerks won't just push paper (or input data at computer terminals): they will become experts on the company's main customers or suppliers, how their systems work, who to deal with there, etc.

Note that the finance department becomes more purely about finance as the company grows. We've already said that the finance controller will take over some of the non-finance jobs that defaulted to the finance cornerstone in the sapling phase. Other such jobs will have new specialists come in and run them.

Office management is one such job, but the most important of them is HR. If our advice was followed, this will have always been done by an external consultant reporting to the finance cornerstone. As the company begins to grow fast, it will need its own in-house HR specialist. Time for an HR director to be bought in. This person should not report to the finance cornerstone, but have their own seat on the board – your people are too important.

Strategy

At the start of the 'young tree' period, strategy remains the same as in the sapling phase: keep correcting to stay on track.

Later, once the company has grown to 100 or more people, you may be faced with one of business's nicer problems – you have actually acquired some serious surplus cash.

At this point, entrepreneurs may start thinking about *taking over other businesses*. We advise against this, unless there is compelling logic (and even then, be very wary). In the world of big business, it's a known fact that most takeovers end up destroying shareholder value. It's also true in the world of smaller businesses.

The real problem is that the things that make takeovers work have nothing to do with markets, figures, assets etc., the kind of topics that will be covered by rational financial analysis. Takeovers only work when the people from both companies gel really well, and this happens quite rarely. Remember: small businesses are tribes, and tribes fight, not merge.

Yes, some companies are good at taking over tiddlers. They have very effective, and well-tested, methodologies both for assessing targets and for integrating them once the takeover has happened.

Hopefully you will be taken over by one of them. Entrepreneurs look at these takeover experts and think 'takeovers are easy', just as after watching a Beckham free kick, you immediately go out into the garden with a football, stub your toe and break a window. Don't be fooled!

Botched takeovers lose money, waste incredible amounts of time and energy, and demotivate staff, who see outsiders promoted above them in the hierarchy and hard-earned money being wasted.

A better use for surplus cash is to expand the business in some way. But even here, be wary. Expansion is best driven by the market – if you're getting a lot of orders from Germany, then follow that through. If you are asking: 'We've got some surplus cash, where can we expand?' you are in danger of expanding into being a solution looking for a problem.

The best way to expand is to have 'intrapreneurs' testing markets quietly, quickly and cheaply. Most of these tests will fail: follow the ones that succeed.

Probably the best uses for surplus cash are the unexciting ones:

★ pay off debts

★ give the staff some kind of treat, or create an incentive scheme for them

★ pay yourselves a dividend

★ keep it in the bank

Funding

We don't, can't, and won't change our basic stance that the best way to fund is from revenue. But we understand that this is not possible for all businesses. Returning to our fixed cost staircase, sometimes the only way forward is a great big leap in costs, and this can usually only be surmounted by cash from outside.

For unavoidable asset purchases, we continue to suggest bank loans secured on those assets. Grants may be available for specific pieces of workforce training or product development. But other types of expansion don't lend themselves to being funded so easily. For example:

★ as you grow, your working capital needs will grow – the 'oil' you need just to keep the wheels of your money-making machine turning

★ you need to take on new people who may not be immediately productive

★ you decide to attack a new market

Banks are unwilling to lend for such expenditures, as there is nothing for them to take away if things go wrong.

Your first recourse, assuming you have not used this facility to the max already, should be to the Small Firms' Loan Guarantee Scheme. Remember that most young tree firms feel huge to the founding team but are 'small' by the standards of government, banks and corporates, so still qualify for this immensely useful scheme.

Once this source of effectively 'unsecured' finance is exhausted, you will have to give away some equity to a business angel, a private investor who will offer money (on average around £50,000; more if you get money from an angel syndicate) for a stake in the business. This is not a disaster. Quite the opposite, actually – as long as you get the right angel.

The wise finance cornerstone (and the wise entrepreneur) makes sure he or she knows about local angel networks: 'local' is important: most angels invest locally. If they have open meetings, he or she should attend one or two, dropping hints – 'things are going well … of course, it's too early for a big tranche of funding yet' – and checking out the various participants.

This last function is the most important. The right angel investor is an invaluable member of the team. They have often made their money in your sector, so they bring invaluable knowledge and contacts to the party (particularly valuable if your finance cornerstone does not have specialist sector knowledge). They are keen to make a good return from their stake, but won't just wander round with their noses stuck in a spreadsheet moaning about return on equity. Remember the Beermat qualifications for a mentor:

★ They like you

★ You like them

★ They get the point of what you are doing

★ They will provide knowledge, contacts and recommendations

This is also true for angels.

The last point above is crucial. Will they pass the 'Golf Club Test', telling their friends about 'this new business they are working with' and thus helping the sales as well as the finance cornerstone by creating leads?

Sadly, as Milton discovered, not all angels are this angelic. 'Fallen angels' have lost the enthusiasm and are really only looking at the figures. They don't put much (or any) time, effort or commitment into the business.

The more you know which local investor falls into which category, the more you will be able to approach the right people when the need for external funding arises.

Naturally, the cost of angel funding falls as the business gets older and more solid. Angels aren't normally interested in pure start-ups, but those that are will want a large stake. It's difficult to quantify how large (somewhere between 35 and 49 per cent). Once the business reaches the sapling phase, the stake required will fall.

The process of getting angel funding can be broken down into steps.

1. *Build mutual respect.* This is a precondition of a good funding deal – in your networking, you have met the angel, and know, like and trust them. Maybe you have even talked to the MDs of some other companies in which the angel has invested, so you know they are the right kind of angel.

2. *Work out how much you really need.* Entrepreneurs often lack a clear picture here. Some overestimate, others underestimate. The finance cornerstone is the person to work out the correct figure.

3. *Work out how much equity you're prepared to give.* This is partially a financial decision, partly an emotional one. Give away too much, and the team become demoralised. Be too stingy, and the angel may flap away to a different cloud.

   Behind this lurk hard facts, or at least hard expectations. What do you think the company will be worth in three years' time? More important, what does the finance cornerstone think the company will be worth in three years' time? Then work back. If you want £x now, assume you'll pay the angel double in three years. So what does that make his or her stake?

   For example, you (and your finance cornerstone) think your business will be worth £1m in three years. Right now you want to raise £50,000. You should be offering an angel an exit worth £2x in three years, which is £100,000 – 10% of what the business will be worth. So offer them that percentage now.

4. *Negotiate.* There's a kind of ritual mating dance you have to go through, like those ones where birds fan their tails, circle round each other and make odd screeching noises (with Sir David Attenborough lurking in the background whispering how marvellous it is). No need to fan your tail: simply ask to meet the angel, and do so with the finance cornerstone.

At the meeting:

★ Ask someone to take notes.

★ Remember, you are not just trying to sell. The angel is selling to you, too. You are offering them a chance of getting involved in a business that will be rewarding to them, both personally and financially. If they don't want this chance, there are other people out there who would welcome the opportunity.

★ At the same time, show that you understand the angel's need for a return and an exit. Don't just enthuse about your business.

★ Be honest. If you are unable to answer a question, tell the angel that you will find out and get back to them.

Discussions will centre round the kinds of calculation above. 'Do you really think you'll be worth £1m? Justify that…'. If you've chosen the right angel, they won't be arguing this in an adversarial fashion (VCs are different), but they will have their own view of your prospects and will want a fair stake.

Just as important are the negotiations about how much involvement the angel will have. Some entrepreneurs like to hear 'none' from the angel, but this is arrogant and foolish. You want to hear the opposite.

If all goes well the process will probably be something like:

★ A request from the angel for more information

★ A further meeting to discuss this info

★ 'Due diligence'. These are more formal investigations by the angel

★ Note – if you haven't checked the angel's record for being the right kind of investor, do so now!

★ A final meeting

★ An initial offer. This is likely to come in the form of a 'term sheet', including an agreement on confidentiality and exclusivity

★ Contract negotiations

★ An agreed offer

5. *Sign!*

6. *Stick to the spirit as well as the letter of the deal.* Good mentor/ angels want to get involved, so make sure they are, and are valued and listened to. Offer them a seat on the board, or the non-exec chairmanship.

The finance cornerstone will have an interesting role to play once the angel is on board. When you were dealing with the bank, the key relationship was between the finance cornerstone and the bank manager. But an angel will probably invest because they like the entrepreneur. This does not mean that the finance cornerstone can vanish into the background. They have to develop a relationship with the angel too, and quietly manage the entrepreneur/angel relationship. This latter role involves ensuring that the entrepreneur always has the right information for the angel. It can mean calming things down if the entrepreneur suddenly terrifies the angel by announcing a new idea they've just had. It's not so much 'good cop, bad cop' as 'fun cop (entrepreneur), dull cop (finance cornerstone)'.

Any other sources of finance?

Don't even think about 'VCs' (Venture Capitalists) yet. They are too ruthless for 'young tree' businesses and the people who run them, and anyway they seem to have lost interest in small companies: if you want anything less than £2m, forget it.

In certain parts of the country, for example former coalfields, the EU and/or UK government have set up various enterprise funds to help local regeneration. These 'soft VCs' will provide more realistic amounts of money, and be less aggressive than commercial VCs in negotiating terms, insisting on stellar growth (etc.). Ask around: someone, somewhere in your region knows all about them – who offers what, who's nice to work with, who suits which kind of business.

Arguably, a better alternative to any VC involvement is if a major stakeholder makes a *strategic investment*. This is usually a customer, who wants to ensure continuity of supply from you. And, if you turn out to have a real, sustainable differentiator, to buy the rest of you later on. More on this in the next chapter.

Cornerstone burnout

As the young tree flourishes, the cornerstones can suffer burnout. They've been working flat out from the beginning. They have lost the tribal world in which they were happiest. Their skills may no longer be appropriate for the size that the company now is – a classic case is the fearless, energetic 'hunter' sales cornerstone who now finds him- or herself stuck behind a spreadsheet trying to do sales management.

The finance cornerstone is the least likely of the team to suffer burnout. First because they probably joined later anyway, so will be less tired, and second because their skills will still be appropriate. So they should be looking for signs of burnout in their fellow board members.

The main signs are the classic ones of stress – illness, erratic behaviour, getting behind with work. The business should have a mentor, who all that time ago helped you get going, and who now keeps a paternal eye on things (no doubt delighted at your success). Talk to them, and suggest they have a word with the cracking-up cornerstone.

The best way to treat cornerstones in this situation is to suggest they take some time off. Lying on a beach or touring cultural relics in Greece, they may decide it's time to walk away. If they don't, then they must be persuaded to go.

The best route out is the 'clean break' – the cornerstone leaves the company, has a rest, then puts their special skills to work again by getting involved in another start-up.

Or they resign both board and operational responsibility, but come in and do work as a consultant.

Alternatively, they could be given a maverick role, starting new projects or working with company intrapreneurs. Steve Jobs did this very successfully at Apple, but his story is unusual. More common is that they take up the role of sniping at the new management from the sidelines – not helpful.

They must retain their special position in the company 'mythology'. Founders are always special.

What is to be done with their stake? Ideally it should be sold, but cornerstones are often unwilling to sell. This is partly because of sentiment, but also because a minority stake in a business isn't worth much (wait till the whole business is sold, and your stake is worth a lot more). In practice a compromise is usually worked out, where some of the stake is bought and the cornerstone keeps the rest – yielding him or her some cash, a residual income, and a promise of more to come when the company is sold.

How to replace them? They may have managers ready (and rather keen) to step into their operational shoes. Fine. In the finance department, the controller may well be ready to step up – but if they're not, find an experienced FD. You'll be large enough now to attract very good people, with experience at building businesses from 100 or more people to something even bigger.

Note that the *entrepreneur* may well burnout, too, as what he or she sees as the rampant bureaucracy of this dull process-driven thing that used to be their exciting company closes ever tighter around them. Wise entrepreneurs spot this coming, and have their own personal exit plan. Others don't, and may need pushing. The finance cornerstone is often the most experienced of the cornerstones, and may have to take the lead in the latter case. He or she should talk to the mentor first, then the other cornerstones. Cornerstones and mentor should jointly tell the entrepreneur it's time to go: they should do so with one voice. (See *The Beermat Entrepreneur* for more on this tricky topic.)

There is another solution to the above problems, however. The company is growing; it passes 150 people – another milestone. For many teams, it is time to sell.

Chapter Eight: **Exit**

Few entrepreneurs give the sale of their business the attention that they should. This reflects both the best and the worst sides of entrepreneurs. Best, insofar as they do business for the love of it – the ideas, the people, the activity – not just as a grey, calculated means to an end. Worst, insofar as they find it hard to imagine the business without them. Louis XIV, whose motto was 'the state is me,' had a mindset shared by many entrepreneurs. (He was in many ways a great ruler: go to Versailles and ponder what this mindset can achieve. But he left chaos behind him: his successor-but-one ended up on the guillotine.)

But most businesses need to be sold at some point. If the business is growing, new skills will be needed at the helm. If it is ticking along but the entrepreneur either wants to do something else or needs to retire, new owners must be found. Thinking about selling is not an optional extra; it's a must.

Selling a business is a process. It needs to be done right, and it takes time. You've worked hard and smart getting the business to where it is: take a little more time and follow some rules to get the benefit you and the rest of the team deserve.

Types of sale

Before we look at the process in depth, we should quickly run over the ways in which owners (entrepreneurs, cornerstones, angels) can exit. We will look at them in (usual) order of shareholder reward.

Management Purchases. A Management Buy-out (MBO) is when the existing managers buy the company. It is a common exit for smaller businesses or where entrepreneurs have kept massive stakes.

Usually the buyers don't put all the cash in upfront: for a £1m company, they might have to stump up £400,000 to start with, and pay the rest later as the company grows, in a series of deferred payments (three more tranches of 20% are common).

MBOs should work well in theory. The existing managers know the business. Ownership will motivate them to build it further. Some MBOs are assisted by finance providers like banks, VCs or (sometimes) angels, so the company gets a useful injection of capital at the same time, too.

However, not every team is right for an MBO. Will they be as good without the entrepreneur in charge? Often the answer is 'no' (Louis XIV-type entrepreneurs are not good at appointing excellent people below them). Even if the team are excellent at what they do now, are they the right people to take the business to its *next* phase? Finally, if extra capital is provided, will the managers get on with the capital provider, or argue and end up demotivated?

Perhaps a better solution is a Management Buy-in (MBI), where external managers, who are experienced specialists at growing young trees into mighty oaks, buy the business and build it. Here, too, extra capital may be put in, but the management/capital provider relationship is usually much better than in MBOs: MBI experts are likely to have a pet capital source with whom they get on well.

The catch is that MBIs are relatively uncommon: there are not many teams of brilliant managers roving round the countryside looking for buy-in opportunities.

There is also a BIMBO, which is a mixture of the above: some existing managers stay, some externals are bought in. It can be a good compromise, though we can't help wondering if the model was created because the acronym was irresistible.

Note that in all these cases, if substantial external capital is put in, the new investors are investing in, and effectively taking control of, the company. They are not paying off the old owners as a kind of thank you for building such a wonderful business. We know this sounds obvious, but it's a point missed by many entre- preneurs. Venture Capitalists in particular will make sure that if the business starts to falter, the first people to lose their stake will be the initial owners. That's you and your team, who are losing your money because the excellent business you built up wasn't able to make it up to the next step.

Trade Sale. For larger young tree businesses, the most common exit route is the Trade Sale, when you are bought by another, almost always larger, business. You tend to get a better price than for an MBO, and a bigger percentage upfront, too.

Take a walk 'round the other side of the table', and consider why a big player might buy you. The answer is that they think they can get more out of your assets than you can. Your business's assets are:

★ Its people

★ Its customers (and its relationship with them)

★ Its market knowledge

★ Any special processes it owns or is a master of, and has proven

★ Its brand(s)

If the buyer is any good at buying, it should be right in thinking it can leverage these. ('Leverage' is an often overused word, but entirely appropriate here. Think of a see-saw, with your assets on one side, and the effort you have to put in to get the best out of them on the other. Lengthen the 'effort' side, then consider the ease with which the new applier of pressure will be able to move those same assets.) A bigger business has greater financial resources; it has tried and tested national (or international) systems for marketing and distribution; it has wider opportunities for your brightest people; it has more products to sell to your favourite customers…

Ideally, the buyer also has a weak spot which you strengthen. For example, a chain of regional estate agents might buy a London agency to complete its UK coverage.

Best of all, you own a 'ransom strip'. The metaphor comes from the property world, where large pieces of property can sometimes only be accessed in one way – and somebody else owns that access. It may be an old track, but suddenly it's worth a fortune to the owner of the site it leads to, who has suddenly been given planning permission. Any monopoly supplier of essential components to an industry is in this fortunate position.

It is these leverage and strategic aspects that mean that you can ask more from a trade buyer.

Trade buyers also tend to be larger companies with solid cashflow, so you can also ask for a bigger percentage of the cash upfront than in a management purchase. You can also be more confident that any future payment tranches will be secure.

The right trade sale, to a buyer who deals hard but fair, pays well and values what they get, is the ideal outcome for an entrepreneur. It happened to Mike, whose company, The Instruction Set, was bought by Hoskyns in the late 1980s. Most 'InSet' people flourished in the new, bigger business (even Mike survived a corporate environment for two years!) and Hoskyns made excellent use of the assets they had acquired.

Any caveats?

Keep one eye open for dodgy buyers. Some 'buyers' may be speculative, hoping to negotiate a price then raise the money: if they fail to do the latter they will have wasted a lot of your time. Others may be trying to get information about you, either to compete more effectively with you, or to find ways of grabbing your key assets (big customers, staff etc.). So if you don't know the buyer, establish if they are serious:

★ Talk to the sellers of any other businesses they have acquired

★ Establish whether they have the financial resources to buy the business. Just ask how any deal would be financed. Later, do a bit of asking around, and take a look at their balance sheet

★ When you plan to meet them, make sure that the person you are dealing with has the authority to acquire businesses

★ When you do meet them, ask lots of open questions about their motives, plans etc. Open questions are ones which require answers containing new information, rather than just 'yes' or 'no'. They begin with how, what, who, why, when or where

★ Don't give away too much information about yourself too soon

But do the above politely: these scenarios are the exception rather than the rule. Most trade buyers are serious, and seriously good news for the shareholders and for the business (and, hopefully, for themselves too).

Initial Public Offering (IPO) is when the company is floated on one of the stock markets. Most small companies that float go onto the Alternative Investment Market (AIM) – a full listing on the main London Stock Exchange is only for large businesses or small ones that are irrationally fashionable, the way the dotcoms were back in 1999. (The exchange says companies floated on the full LSE must have a turnover of at least £700,000 'but are normally a lot larger'.)

IPO is a process that suits some entrepreneurs – the ones that are very motivated financially, and who start a business with one eye on the public markets. They may get VCs on board part way through the process, and should get on well with the VCs, who have a similar focus.

For other entrepreneurs – the visionaries, the doers-from-love-of-doing – IPO tends to be pretty hellish. You now have to dance to the tunes of City investors, many of whom think incredibly short term. You are subject to a host of new regulations. And your new wealth is still largely on paper. Yes, you will still have a nice chunk of equity. But you won't be allowed to sell this chunk for some while (most IPOs allow *some* shares to be sold as part of the offering, so you won't be penniless; but you'll have to sit on most of your paper wealth for a long and nerve-racking time).

Note also that IPO is a purely financial exit. Unlike all the other routes above where you move on, the entrepreneur and corner-stones will be expected to remain at the helm of the floated business for quite a while.

The biggest advantage to IPO is price. You can get twice what a trade sale would realise (unless your trade buyer has an over-whelming strategic need to take you over), because when you become a quoted company your shares will be much more marketable and thus more valuable. Another advantage is that you can issue more shares to buy other businesses (be careful!), to raise further capital via 'rights' issues, or (very important) to motivate employees via share schemes.

No exit. There is, of course, a final alternative to all the above routes – not to exit at all, just keep on building the business.

Very few entrepreneurs have what it takes both to start a business and to run a corporation. So if they want to see their young tree grow into a mighty and still privately-owned oak, they must back off, handing the business over to a new generation of managers and simply becoming 'rentiers', collecting an ever-increasing dividend cheque every six months. This is hard for most entrepreneurs to do, and we feel that a clean break involving transfer of ownership is better. If you've sold the business to Megacorp, or to your managers, you can't sneak back into the boss's office and sit in that chair.

Those few entrepreneurs, like Richard Branson, who remain bosses of their now-massive companies tend to be very good at delegating (not the strong suit of most entrepreneurs). They actually become figureheads, a bit like royal families in modern constitutional monarchies, who do lots of ceremonial/PR work, high-level networking, and general morale-raising among the troops, but have long ago ceded their decision-making power to other institutions. Such a role is not easy to play (the celeb bit is easy; it's the hands-off bit that's tough).

The sale process

We will slant this narrative towards owners seeking trade buyers, as that is the route we both recommend and find most common. However most of the steps are relevant to all types of exit: proper grooming, intelligent courtship of the right buyer, the Beermat Buyer's Pack...

In the last chapter we talked about the process of finding an angel. The process of finding a buyer has a lot in common with it. Finding a buyer is another one of these ritual dances, but it lasts a lot longer and needs more planning. Birds just dance from instinct: this is a ballet you have to choreograph.

As with all processes, it needs to be broken down into a number of steps. These are largely, but not totally, sequential:

★ Think 'buyer' from early on

★ Decide to sell

★ Groom

★ Establish a value in your own mind

★ Court/seek buyers

★ Get a serious reply and make the right responses to it

★ The indicative offer

★ Negotiation

★ The final offer

★ Due diligence

★ Beginning to reveal the secret

★ Memorandum of Sale

★ Sign!

★ Tell the world

★ Move on

Think buyer from early on. As we've said, few entrepreneurs do this. They build and run the business, then suddenly decide to sell. More savvy entrepreneurs will give this matter thought earlier on. Not right at the start – you have to get the business up and running first – but once it is growing and clearly has potential. Who might want to buy you? Think of your assets, especially the intangible ones like intellectual property (IP), skills, brand, reputation, customer relations: to whom would these be of *most* use?

Once you've gone through this thought process, you should start the courtship at once, even if it's far, far too early to actually sell the business to them. (Think of those costume dramas where, near the end, the hero says to the heroine something along the lines of 'I have long regarded you as a friend, Miss X, but recently my feelings have undergone a most remarkable transformation...' You want to hear similar sentiments from Megacorp in three years' time.)

Make sure you are a supplier to the chosen buyer, preferably providing them with something nobody else provides quite as well. Or get involved in some kind of joint venture with them.

You could go further if you feel like it: can you persuade Megacorp to take a strategic stake in you? This will provide some capital (always handy), and prime them for buying you when the time is right. (Make sure the stake does not limit your options in dealing with Megacorp's rivals.)

A finance cornerstone is more likely to 'think buyer' early on than an entrepreneur. Indeed, the entrepreneur might well resent the finance cornerstone thinking this way: there's a whiff of treason about it. The finance cornerstone should stick to their line. They will be thanked for it later.

Decide to sell. Wiser entrepreneurs know that their skill lies in the stages of business we have described in this book: seedling, sapling, young tree. They also understand the above material about why a big player would want to buy them. So the case for selling becomes clearer and clearer as the business grows. However there is usually a moment when the decision 'crystallises' – we know several entrepreneurs who have said, 'I just woke up one morning and knew it was time to sell'.

The decision is often prompted by the emergence of a problem on the horizon. These are often problems that could be solved easily by a bigger company; for example, if a large chunk of capital expenditure will become necessary. So selling is not a cop-out, but a logical, sensible step.

The worst decisions to sell are those forced on entrepreneurs by immediate circumstances. In truth, circumstances on their own are rarely enough – normally entrepreneurs overcome adversity and rather enjoy doing so. Entrepreneurs 'forced to sell' have usually allowed themselves to drift into boredom. Maybe a new idea has taken their fancy. Suddenly, something goes wrong, for example the defection of a key customer (who may have noticed the loss of spark from the business). The entrepreneur suddenly wants out.

It's almost impossible to sell a business for anything other than a knock-down price under these circumstances. If you are an entrepreneur in this position, steel yourself for 'one more push' to bring the business back to life. You will need to inject some new vigour into the process – get someone with turnaround expertise on board.

Manna from heaven

The decision to sell can be made for you, via an unexpected offer. If this comes out of the blue rather than from a partner you have been quietly courting for a while, check that it is serious. But such offers usually are serious, and good offers too: the buyer thinks you have something they need, and will be prepared to pay a premium, often 20 per cent over an independent valuation.

▶▶

Check to see if there are any other potential buyers before granting exclusivity. The finance cornerstone should have some civilised lunches with the top finance people of the suitor's rivals (or anyone else considered to be buyer material). Mention you've received an offer. Don't say who from, and don't drop hints. Ask them if they are interested.

A similar lunch with a company broker (see below) would be worth having too. As would a subscription to a gym after all these lunches.

⌐Beermat.biz

Grooming. When you decide to sell, don't rush out and stick a 'For Sale' board outside the business. Even if you have a preferred buyer you are close to, it's now time to prepare the company for sale, just as you would make your house look nice before putting it on the market. This isn't about cheating the buyer by hiding things, but about making your business as tidy and buyable as possible:

★ Obtain long-term commitment from customers and suppliers. Happy customers will often be delighted to sign contracts for longer periods of time – you are ensuring them continuity of supply. Suppliers will naturally be delighted to sign you up for longer. At the same time, avoid over-dependence on key customers and suppliers. If you are over-dependent – get selling and sourcing!

★ Focus on current and medium-term profits. This doesn't mean become like the worst kind of City fund manager and think quarter by quarter, but it does mean deferring plans that have a long pay-off time. Be sceptical about starting new growth initiatives, unless the market is screaming at you to make them. (If you feel there is a new, sudden, once-in-a-lifetime opportunity for the business, put the sale plan on ice and go for it.) Batten down the hatches and make sure you are doing what you do now as well as possible.

★ Minimise *any* long-term commitment to costs. Again, this should be standard practice in the Beermat business, with its maxim of 'stay flexible'. The issue is even more important now.

★ Sell underused assets. That way, you get the benefit. If the assets aren't important, their absence probably won't have much effect on the price – a bit like odd bits of furniture you inherit when you buy a house.

★ Cut any other flab. Is everyone in the organisation pulling their weight? In Beermat companies, the answer is usually 'yes'. But now is a good time to check.

★ Keep the rest of the team on board and motivated. Make sure that the best people now stay with the business up to (and beyond) your sale. Revamp the bonus scheme. Grant share options, exercisable if the company is sold.

★ Make sure the legal coast is clear. This means among other things: talk to a solicitor, settle any litigation or disputes hanging over the company's head, make sure everyone's employment contracts (and directors' agreements) are up to date, and that there is a shareholders' agreement in place.

★ Ensure you are up to date with Health and Safety compliance.

★ If you do not do so already, get audited accounts.

Readers won't be surprised to hear us say that the finance cornerstone is the right person to take responsibility for this process. The entrepreneur must oversee it and value it, but the finance person is the one to ensure it gets carried out in detail.

As well as the above, there are two pieces of common sense not strictly about grooming but which matter at this period:

★ Plan ahead now to ensure that your tax liability on sale is minimised. You can save a fortune by getting this right, but it is very complex and very specialist. We won't go into the details: speak to the best expert you can find.

★ Don't disengage from the business. This is crucial: we've seen it happen often. Entrepreneurs start thinking about villas in Barbados – and, bang!, they've lost the passion and drive that will actually provide these things for them. Stay at the helm of your business, and you'll end up with a real yacht.

The grooming process can take up to a year. Let it: you are building value.

Establish a value in your own mind. Now that the company is neatly groomed for sale, how much is it worth? The answer, of course, is 'what someone will pay for it'. This you can only guess. Make the guess as informed as possible by establishing a 'base price' and working up from that.

The most basic valuation method is simply to tot up the net assets of the business. Harsh, but it may be used on you if the sale is made for the wrong reasons and the business is struggling. However, you have planned and groomed, so you should not suffer this.

More common is to base the valuation on a multiple of earnings. This multiple is called the price/earnings (= p/e) ratio. For quoted companies, p/e ratios are listed on the share-prices pages of the FT (or other quality papers). Take the market capitalisation (total value of all shares) of a company then divide that by the company's profit after tax. For example, if Megacorp have 1,000 million shares in issue, and the share price is £4.40, and they made £350 million last year, their p/e is:

$$\frac{1,000,000,000 \times 4.4}{350,000,000} = 12.57$$

Note that p/e ratios tend to be reasonably constant across sectors, though not across the whole market: looking at the FT as we write this, the average p/e of construction companies is 10, while the software and computer services sector is valued at 25 times earnings.

Find the quoted company most like you. What is its p/e? Unless you're going for IPO, divide this figure by half to get a reasonable multiplier for an unquoted company.

All this sounds easy, but the problem really comes with establishing earnings. Simple, surely? Profit after tax… But does this figure tell the full story? Is the business being run for profit, or to subsidise the owner/manager lifestyle? Also, profit over what period? One year's accounts may contain one-off events like asset sales or just reflect a lucky year. The finance cornerstone of any potential buyer will be going through your accounts with a toothcomb, trying to work out a figure for what he or she will call 'normalised' and 'maintainable' earnings – money made from normal business activities, assuming sensible management expenses, that are likely to recur (or increase) in the future. You should know what this figure is: base your calculations on that.

Going down the management purchase route, the formula 'normalised and maintainable earnings x the appropriate multiplier' is pretty much what the company is worth. A trade buyer should pay more if you have something special that they want and only you can provide. Of course, you must be realistic here. How special is what you've got? The answer may well be 'very special to buyer x, reasonably special to buyer y and not at all special to buyer z'.

Courting and finding buyers. If you've been 'thinking buyer' from early on, you will have been doing this. Well done. Sadly, many entrepreneurs don't; but it's not too late. Think buyer now. Who has a close relationship with you, who would be damaged if you disappeared or were bought by a rival? Who could make the most of the assets you have now? In other words, who is the 'buyer x' in the example above?

For a business that has given no thought to selling but has suddenly decided to sell – or for the company that has tried courting chosen buyers but failed to get a response – you have to get yourself in front of as many potential buyers as possible. Not so much courtship as speed dating.

Prepare a one-page document about yourself, a bit like those brochures you get from an estate agent providing the basic details of the property (the big difference is that yours should be anonymous). The one-pager should reveal:

★ The company's elevator pitch – the pain you solve, who for, and why people buy from you rather than rivals.

★ The opportunity for the buyer. If the company is selling because it knows it needs outside help/finance to move the next step up, then say so. If the buyer believes instead that the business is up for sale because the entrepreneur simply wants out (is bored, wants lots of money now etc.), then they'll either lose interest or drive the price down.

★ A generic list of clients (i.e. just say 'UK banks' not 'Lloyds TSB and Barclays').

★ Basic financials. Turnover, approx gross and net margins. Highlight the good points – low borrowings, healthy cash-flow, substantial asset backing, upward sales trend (or whatever).

Initially, talk to contacts, especially professionals who interact with other businesses: your accountants, your lawyers, your bank. The finance cornerstone is a) most likely to have these contacts and b) the right person to do this: he or she will appear to be, and will be, more objective. The finance cornerstone may well have industry contacts, too.

These chats should reveal a number of companies known to be keen to make acquisitions. Get whoever forms the bridge between the finance cornerstone and the potential buyer (i.e. the accountant/lawyer/banker who suggested them) to make a formal introduction. The finance cornerstone should then contact the buyer direct, with the one-pager.

At the same time, talk to company brokers like Company Exchange (www.thecompanyexchange.com) or Avondale (www.avondale-group.co.uk). Like estate agents, brokers will find and screen buyers, and get paid commission on sale only. They will also 'hold your hand' during the negotiation process, though an experienced finance cornerstone should not need this.

Their cost is around 2% of the deal (and a minimum of around £25,000). Brokers will also charge for preparing documents like the Information Memorandum (see below): do these yourself.

The outcome of all this flirtation and self-advertisement should be a *serious reply*. The dance moves on!

If necessary, check out the buyer as much as you can. In a negative way, to make sure they are serious, but (more important) in a positive way, to think how much value you could add to their business.

The entrepreneur and finance cornerstone should meet with the interested acquisition team. If you get a bad feeling about them, back off. If you get a good feeling – still take care, but it's a good sign. Money will be discussed, but only in ballpark terms.

If you are both still serious after this, it's time to request a Non-Disclosure Agreement (NDA), as you are about to reveal confidential information.

Once this is signed, it is time to open up to the buyer: if you hold back now, they will think you're hiding something. Prepare an Information Memorandum. This is essentially an up-to-date version of your current business plan, with any sensitive details removed and perhaps a few details gone into in greater depth (the ones that make you look good). A SWOT analysis (i.e. of your strengths, weaknesses, opportunities and threats) makes a good addition, too.

Rather than send it to them, why not turn it into a PowerPoint presentation and have the finance cornerstone deliver it in person? It will give him or her the opportunity to get a good look at the buyer, as well as to enthuse about your business.

However it's delivered, the buyer will ponder the Info Memorandum, then you will meet again for them to fire questions at you about it. As usual, be honest. If the questions wander into sensitive areas, such as details of your relationship with specific customers or of processes/IP unique to the company, say you can't answer them yet. If it's a legitimate question but you don't know the answer, say you'll get back to them. And get back to them. If they want to look at management accounts, let them.

Discuss the 'Rules of Engagement'. Who talks to whom? It should be finance cornerstone to finance cornerstone. What's the time limit within which an offer, or a 'no thanks', should be delivered? Two weeks is standard and reasonable.

Note the pivotal role of the finance cornerstone in all this. The entrepreneur will want to be involved, but it is better if the minutiae are sorted by the finance specialist. Remember that a good finance cornerstone will have been through this experience before, and that he or she will know perfectly well that the ultimate decision is the entrepreneur's.

Keep meetings friendly and informal – but, as with angel meetings, have someone take notes. Circulate them to all parties after the event.

Both sides should then do more research: at the end of the agreed period, an *Indicative Offer* should follow.

This will outline a proposal to buy your business subject to 'due diligence' (see below). The document will still be brief, running to three or four pages and covering:

★ the price and terms

★ an intended completion date

★ exclusivity (and penalties to be incurred if you suddenly sell to someone else)

★ confidentiality

★ the expected roles of the entrepreneur and cornerstones, post-acquisition

There will also be a clause about what you now can not do in terms of changing prices, taking on new liabilities and other major business changes. Note, control is already slipping out of your hands…

The negotiation now enters its crucial phase. The main debate will be about price and terms.

The entrepreneur will believe the business to be worth x. The finance cornerstone is the person to marshal and present the arguments behind that valuation, and to defend those arguments when they are criticised.

But don't forget payment terms. Just as when you started out, think cash. In practice, there will be some element of deferred payment in the deal. There always is. But try to minimise it.

Especially, try and avoid 'earn-outs', where the deferred payment is conditional on the company adding such-and-such an amount of value over a period of, say, two years. It's understandable that the buyer wants to make some of the money they are paying you dependent on the company turning out to have been a good buy. But your control over things will be limited from the moment of sale, so the running of the business is no longer up to you. Why should you bet some of the value you are receiving for your business on how somebody else runs it in the next two years?

Remember also that you are being an honest and open seller. There are no tricks up your sleeve. That's the Beermat way, the way of ethical, 'win-win' business. Large earn-out clauses are the product of distrustfulness, which in turn is the product of the 'zero-sum game' approach to business (i.e. there is always a winner and a loser).

Insist on legally binding payment guarantees for those deferred payments that you have to concede. This is particularly important with management buy-outs – get personal guarantees from the purchasers.

There may be some room for debate about the old owners' role in the new company. We recommend the 'clean break', but be aware that it won't be 100% clean (unless the takeover is hostile, a relatively rare event with unlisted companies): you will be required to work with the new business to hand over.

These negotiations may well take a couple of months, and involve amended versions of the offer being passed back between you and the buyer like one of those long tennis rallies – on clay, between two baseline players. Be patient. If you are the finance cornerstone, be extra patient, as the entrepreneur will be on edge, eager (to keep the tennis metaphor going) to rush up to the net and try and force an error. They should not do this. It's risky.

While this is going on, it is imperative that the business keeps going. You don't want anything going wrong now! You can also do a bit of last-minute tidying up. Contact any debtors and push for payment. If they can't pay right now, get a promise to pay (on company notepaper) from them. If they really are hopeless cases, write them off.

Finally, price, terms and any other details will be agreed, and a *Final Offer* will be made.

This is progress, but the game isn't over yet. The offer is still 'subject to *due diligence*'.

Due diligence is the legal phrase for the buyer's investigations into your business. They are supposed to exercise due (i.e. appropriate) diligence in investigating the potential purchase, and if they don't, then they are at fault if something later goes wrong. (You, the seller, are expected to exercise similar diligence in being truthful to them.) The meaning has migrated from a description of the way the process should be carried out to the name of the process itself, a bit like the word 'jolly' now means an event that is supposed to be jolly, like a works outing. (On this principle, some corporate occasions ought to be called 'miserables'.)

Due diligence is not particularly jolly. It's meticulous and time-consuming – a standard length of time for it is two months. Entrepreneurs often get nervous during this time, not because they have hidden things, but because they're naturally impetuous. 'Just get on with it!' The finance cornerstone is the right person to calm them down, and remind them that due diligence is slow but essential.

It is carried out into all areas of the business: financial, legal, commercial, technological.

If any one of these reveals 'holes', negotiations will open up again. The analogy with a formal offer for a house is appropriate here: the surveyor still has to come in, and may well find things that will be used as a lever to get the price down.

Rather obviously, if they discover something unexpectedly nice, they won't say 'Hey, we'll pay you extra for this'. So your arguments from here on will be defensive, against attempts to argue the price down. Your best defence against these is having been scrupulously honest in all your communications with the buyer. That way if they turn round and say 'here's a problem; we want £100,000 off the price', you can point out that they have already been told about it.

As with the Information Memorandum, follow the old marketing adage and 'make it easy for the customer to buy'. We recommend preparing what we call the Beermat Buyer's Pack, which contains all the information and documentation the buyer needs. It can take a month to assemble, but can end up as one CD plus some boxes of photocopies. It can save your buyer a huge amount of time, create goodwill between you and save wasting time haggling over uncertainties – but, of course, its greatest benefit is as a defence against attacks on the price.

The person to prepare the buyer's pack is, of course, the finance cornerstone. As with the Real Business Plan, sections will reflect the work of other cornerstones, but the buck for this kind of thing stops at the desk marked 'finance'.

The Beermat Buyer's pack

★ The Memorandum and Articles of Association

★ The shareholders' agreement

★ A more detailed technical description of your products/services

★ The actual paperwork behind your IP

★ Five years' accounts (if you've been going that long). Balance sheet, P and L, cash flow, tax returns

★ A precise forecast for next year's accounts

★ A rough forecast for the next three years' accounts

★ An estimate of this year's tax liability

★ Any outstanding issues with the taxman

★ A list of aged (longstanding) debtors and what you are doing about them

★ A list of major clients, and the details of your contracts with them

★ Documentation of any leases

★ Proof of ownership of properties, and an independent valuation of them (with the name and contact details of the valuer)

▶▶

★ List all employees, plus job titles, when they joined and severance details (in other words, what it would cost the new owner to fire them; something you hope won't happen, but something the buyer needs to know)

★ Employee contracts

★ Details of share options and other incentive schemes

★ Director service agreements

★ Any outstanding litigation or customer disputes

Beermat.biz

It's now time to *start letting the secret out.*

Up till now, the only people to know about the sale are the entrepreneur and cornerstones, plus the company's mentor and/or chairman. But when you send the 'buyer's pack', the buyer will naturally send people to your premises to check it. Rumours will start to fly, and rumour is always destructive of morale. The secret must no longer be kept.

Time for entrepreneurial leadership. Get everyone in a room, and break the news. You don't need to – and should not – name the company. You should say:

★ that negotiations are underway to a buyer

★ that you can't reveal their name at the moment ('So don't try and force it out of me!')

★ that you approve of them as a buyer. Explain why the deal is a win-win for both sides: they get the assets to leverage, we get the value of their capital, markets (or whatever the synergy in the deal is)

★ that the company needs this deal to carry on growing. The alternative is not trundling along but going into decline

★ that the buyer wants the existing people to be part of the future (assuming this is true)

★ remind them that their share options will be exercised on sale, meaning they will benefit financially from the sale

In reality, you will get a range of responses. Shock may be the initial one – it was when the Griffiths brothers announced that The Instruction Set was being sold. Many people will also feel sad, which is a great tribute to the entrepreneur and cornerstones, as it shows you have made this a great place to work.

Later, as the news sinks in, feelings will divide into two camps. One group will be excited by the opportunities open to them in a new, bigger company. The other will be fearful, unwilling to leave the cheerful, semi-tribal atmosphere of the entrepreneurial young tree business and afraid their jobs will be on the line.

The entrepreneur should talk, one-to-one, to as many of your people as he or she can.

The sales cornerstone should have a chat with all the main customers, assuring them of continuity of supply, both during the negotiation period and from the new owner.

The operations cornerstone should talk to key suppliers, assuring them of similar continuity.

While the due diligence process is going on, solicitors for both parties will prepare a *Memorandum of Sale*. Lawyers are trained to cover every eventuality; hence the length (and cost) of this document.

An important part of it will be the warranties and indemnities. As sellers, you will be asked to warrant (guarantee) a set of statements about the business: that all debts are collectable, that you have no disputes with HMRC (and so on). The indemnities give these force – they state what you will pay if the warranted claims turn out to be false.

As with all areas of sales, negotiation about these can be protracted. Some points:

★ Put a cap on indemnities, on each one individually and on the aggregate amount you are liable for. The buyer will want potential indemnities to be as large as possible; you want them to be tiny.

★ The buyer will also want warranties to last as long as possible – again, negotiate this period down.

★ Have *de minimis* restrictions (ones that limit any claims to reasonable amounts of money). You don't want to waste time arguing over £257.85.

★ Do not warrant anything that is not a known fact – e.g. any projections.

★ The above includes things you might know, but don't. For example, a buyer might ask for some guarantee that nobody else is working on a product like yours. You can only promise to be honest and say that you don't know of anyone. If a chap you've never heard of in Sydney turns out to be a direct rival a year later – well, that's business.

★ Work with lawyers on this – don't try to DIY!

After a little posturing, buyers almost always see reason on these issues. And in fact most warranties never get called in anyway.

Finally, it's time to *sign*. Everything's been sorted; you'll just pop over to the lawyers, get out the special pen you bought for the occasion, write your name – and it's done!

In your dreams! You need to go into the signing session in peak condition, armed with all the facts and ready for a long, hard final bargaining session. Now is *not* the time to relax!

Buyers may chuck in a big curveball. 'We've suddenly noticed x…' Suddenly? Oh yeah. But play straight, answer with facts, don't be browbeaten.

The debate at this point is less likely to be about price, but about other aspects like terms, warranties or indemnities. Don't fall into the trap of regarding these as trivial.

Even if the buyer plays by purest Queensberry rules, the lawyers will do their best to string things out. Cynics will point out they are being paid by the hour 'or part thereof'. Add to this the fact that most commercial lawyers are competitive types: getting two sets of them in one room is a bit like putting two of those Siamese fighting fish in one bowl (come back an hour later, and there's one). To be fair to the lawyers, they are also there to iron out the tiniest inconsistency – that's their job. Whatever the rights and wrongs, the entrepreneur is likely to find this particularly frustrating: once again the finance cornerstone will probably find themselves having to act as calmer-in-chief.

Our top tip for speeding up the signing session is not to let any single issue take up too much time. Instead, if the lawyers are really getting stuck into a topic, suggest it be left for the moment but noted down on a 'to sort later' list, and that you move on to the next topic and/or adjourn for yet another cup of coffee.

The benefits of this are twofold.

★ Your subconscious mind will ponder the problem, and when you come back to it, both you and the buyer may have a new perspective on it.

★ The outcome of this process will probably be a list of a few contentious points. Rather than fight tooth and nail over every one, it is much better to agree to concede some and stand your ground on others. This compromise will be made in the context of the deal as a whole – a better perspective than when you are arguing about a specific.

Another useful hint is 'get it all done in one sitting'. The comment about the subconscious above might lead on to the idea that you should at some point stop the negotiations, call it a day and sleep on it. Don't. It's a very good idea to take a break and go for a walk round the block, but once everyone is there in the room, get the deal done.

One entrepreneur we know had everything drawn up, came to the solicitors, sat down – and did nothing. He just sat there, paralysed, then called the deal off. When asked why, he said, 'I just couldn't sign.'

Please don't do this! Go through everything very thoroughly, and if there is anything with which you are still unhappy, discuss it with the buyer.

Probably the main feeling *after you sign* will be exhaustion. But there'll be elation, too – you should now be worth an amount of money most of your fellow citizens can only dream of. Millionaire… that word has a nice sound to it, doesn't it? Go and buy something nice. Not ridiculously expensive, but something that will later remind you of how good it felt to have just sold… because this mood rarely lasts. Marketing people talk about 'cognitive dissonance', by which they mean those recriminations that set in once you've made a purchase. 'Was I right, after all? Should I have done y instead of that z the lawyers kept going on about?' Apparently much car advertising is aimed at calming this instinctive reaction. Yes, you were right to buy our Super De Luxe Sport – look, here's a bloke with a gorgeous blonde/woman with a hunk driving one along the French Riviera...

Some tips for handling this strange phenomenon:

★ Don't ruminate about that one point on which you conceded and which you now realise was a mistake. It probably matters a lot less than you are telling yourself now. Remind yourself that *no deal is perfect*: if the deal was 'pretty fair', then you've done fine.

★ Mourn the old company. All societies have ceremonies to mark personal passage and loss: create one for what is oddly like a bereavement. Have a wake, a pub evening for the entire team, with all drinks on the now-rich sellers. Make it a rule that people can say whatever's on their mind at this occasion. Remember the nice comments, forget the negative ones.

★ The change has effects on people around you, too. Prepare for this. You will find some people you thought were friends may turn odd. They suddenly want money off you, and get stroppy if you don't provide it. 'I've got this amazing idea for a film, it'll only cost £25,000, you've got all this money... You won't give it to me? You stingy ★★★! (insert rude word of your choice)'. Ditch people like this. At the same time, do share your good luck with real friends.

★ In the end, time, and the emergence of new challenges, makes cognitive dissonance go away.

You will now need to tell your people the full details of the sale. It's also time to call the rest of your customers and suppliers, with the same message you told your key ones earlier – business as usual.

Then it's time to *leave*.

In practice, you won't leave at once. There will be a period of 'knowledge transfer'. This is particularly important for the cornerstones, whose knowledge of their part of the business is specific.

Some deals commit the cornerstones, or even the entrepreneur and cornerstones, to sticking around for anything from 18 months to two years. In our experience, these tend not to work. The job of the departing owners should be to impart their knowledge then depart.

Much better to have a more general clause about your 'being available to support' the business during a transition period, together with the inevitable 'non-compete' clause.

When you do leave, follow a proper 'personal exit procedure':

★ Take a break. Go and do something different, preferably in a new location. That travelling you always wanted to do. And learn scuba-diving or study local history when you're there…

★ When you get back, make a vow not to invest in any businesses for six months.

★ Get networking again. If you find something that attracts you, do some mentoring for nothing. Start building new contacts, new knowledge.

★ When these new contacts and knowledge are considerable, *then* it's time to think about your next big project. Another business? Something more personal? (Mike founded, and toured the UK with, a band after selling The Instruction Set.) 'Putting something back' via social entrepreneurship?

Exits on a Beermat

(beats a magic carpet any day…)

★ Groom the company

★ Court the right buyer

★ Help them buy

★ Get out and let them get on with building to the next stage

★ Follow a 'personal exit procedure'

Beermat.biz

Conclusion

So there it is – the business idea that you had in the pub all those years ago has just turned into a large cheque.

It's important to keep the last chapter in context. Many businesses don't sell for a fortune. Nor do they crash spectacularly, Enron-style. Instead, they plough along making money for the owners, providing work for their people and solving customer pain. This is a fine outcome – well done to anyone who achieves this.

In both cases, the big sale or the successful-but-small ongoing business, finance plays a key part in getting it right. We hope we have shown that finance is not something to fear, but something to understand, use and even enjoy. It's a set of attitudes, a way of thinking, a discipline that makes life easier. No, business is ultimately not about money but about passion, people, hard work, hard choices and above all happy customers. But sound financial thinking and practice underlie all these things, and turn them all into something that lasts, flourishes and serves its purpose in the real world.

Busy-ness to business: good luck with your journey.

Appendices

Appendix A: Model Statutory Accounts

These accounts follow a strict standard format. The rather pompous wording (like 'dividends absorbing £10,000', which just means 'dividends of £10,000', or 'directors' emoluments') is standard, too.

We'd love to be able to explain how some of these expressions arise – but have no idea! They just have.

The key is not to be afraid of them. Finance cornerstones will treat them as 'boilerplate', as a template for the relevant figures.

FUTURA GADGETS LTD

Company No. 09876543

DIRECTORS' REPORT

The directors present their report with the accounts of the company for the year ended 31st December 2004. This report has been prepared in accordance with the special provisions relating to small companies within Part VII of the Companies Act 1985.

Principal Activity
The principal activity of the company in the year under review was that of manufacture of electronic goods.

Results and Dividend
There was a profit for the year after taxation amounting to £15,000. The Directors recommend payment of dividends absorbing £10,000, leaving £5,000 retained.

Directors
The directors in office during the year under review together with their beneficial interests in the shares of the company were as follows:

	Ordinary shares of £1 each	
	31st December 2004	31st December 2003
Mr T Tura	2,000	2,000
Mr F Fu	2,000	2,000
Ms I N Ventor	2,000	2,000
Mr A Charm	2,000	2,000
Mr H Beantrimmer	2,000	2,000

On behalf of the board of Futura Gadgets Ltd:

T Tura, Secretary
31st August, 2005

Notes on various entries in the main accounts follow. All are standard; some are more useful than others!

Note yet another definition of profit – *operating profit*, profit before deduction of interest (or adding any interest you have been paid). This is also known as PBIT, Profit Before Interest and Tax.

The *statement of recognised gains and losses* relates to gains or losses not made through the company's normal business. The classic example is a paper gain from the revaluation of a property (unless you're a property company, of course!).

Such a gain (or loss) would not be put through the P and L account, but go straight into the balance sheet.

Futura Gadgets Ltd
PROFIT AND LOSS ACCOUNT
for the year ended 31st December 2004

	2004	2003
	£'000	£'000
Turnover – *note 2*	1,400	1,300
Cost of sales	(900)	(850)
Gross profit	500	450
Distribution costs	(40)	(38)
Administrative expenses	(430)	(412)
Operating profit/(loss) – *note 3*	30	—
Interest receivable/(payable)	(10)	(10)
Profit/(loss) on ordinary activities before taxation	20	(10)
Tax on profit on ordinary activities – *note 4*	(5)	—
Profit/(loss) for the financial year after taxation	15	(10)
Dividends paid and proposed	(10)	—
Retained profit/(loss) for the financial year	5	(10)

STATEMENT OF RECOGNISED GAINS AND LOSSES
for the year ended 31st December 2004

The company had no recognised gains or losses other than the results for the year as set out above.

The *called up share capital* is the nominal value of the shares that have been issued. This value is usually £1, but doesn't have to be. As 10,000 Futura shares with a £1 nominal value have been issued, the called up share capital is £10,000...

...but in fact, the shareholders have put in more money than this. They have put in £225,000 of their own money. The stat accounts assume they paid the nominal value for their shares, then put in some extra money – the latter is shown in this *share premium account.*

Some accounts will also include a *revaluation reserve*, along with the three categories here. If Futura's £200,000 property was suddenly revalued at £500,000, the new value would be placed in the balance sheet under 'fixed assets', and the gain of £300,000 would appear in this reserve. (The revaluation would also be mentioned in the 'Statement of Recognised Gains' earlier.)

Remember the rule that small companies do not require formal audit. Futura has taken advantage of this.

True does not mean perfectly true, but free from 'material' errors (i.e. errors that would make a difference to a potential investor).

Futura Gadgets Ltd
BALANCE SHEET as at 31st December 2004

	2004		2003	
	£'000	£'000	£'000	£'000
FIXED ASSETS				
Tangible assets – *note 5*	290		320	
		290		320
CURRENT ASSETS				
Stocks – *note 6*	145		125	
Debtors – *note 7*	210		180	
Cash at bank and in hand	10		5	
	365		310	
CREDITORS: amounts falling due within one year – *note 8*	(220)		(200)	
NET CURRENT ASSETS		145		110
CREDITORS: amounts falling due after more than one year		–		–
TOTAL ASSETS LESS CURRENT LIABILITIES		435		430
CAPITAL AND RESERVES				
Called up share capital – *note 9*		10		10
Share premium account		215		215
Profit and loss account – *note 10*		210		205
SHAREHOLDERS' FUNDS		435		430

These accounts have been prepared in accordance with the special provisions relating to smaller companies within Part VII of the Companies Act 1985 and with the Financial Reporting Standard for Smaller Entities (effective June 2002).

The directors consider that the company is entitled to exemption from the requirement to have an audit under section 249A(1) of the Companies Act 1985. Shareholders holding 10% or more of the nominal value of the company's issued share capital have not issued a notice requiring an audit under section 249B.

The directors acknowledge their responsibility for ensuring that the company keeps accounting records which comply with section 221 of the Companies Act 1985, and for preparing accounts which give a true and fair view of the state of affairs of the company as at 31st December 2004 and of its profit for the year then ended in accordance with the requirements of section 226, and which otherwise comply with the requirements of the Act relating to the accounts so far as applicable to the company.

On behalf of the board of Futura Gadgets Ltd:

T Tura, Director
31st August 2005

Historical cost accounting was a big issue in the Seventies, an era of ridiculous inflation (both financial and tonsorial). For a while companies were urged to adjust their accounts for the effect of this inflation. Exactly how this was to be done created acrimonious debate in the profession (and between the profession and industry). Finally, a standard was agreed on, but luckily by this time the root cause of the problem was in decline, as governments around the world started taking inflation seriously and rooting it out. With a sigh of relief, accountants returned to the original convention, the one used here, of simply recording transactions at cost.

Emoluments, are, of course, pay.

Deferred taxation is more of an issue for large companies – which is just as well, as few people understand its intricacies. It relates to tax liabilities that may be payable in the future. For example if a property is revalued, the value goes straight into the balance sheet. No tax is payable on this, but if the building were to be sold in the future for this new price, tax would be payable on the profit. Accountants, being cautious creatures, put an assessment of how much this tax might be in the existing accounts.

Futura Gadgets Ltd
NOTES TO THE ACCOUNTS

1) Accounting policies

Accounting convention
The accounts have been prepared under the historical cost convention and in accordance with the Financial Reporting Standard for Smaller Entities (effective June 2002).

Turnover
Turnover represents the net invoiced sales of goods, excluding Value Added Tax.

Tangible fixed assets
Depreciation is provided at an annual rate of 20% to write off each asset over its useful economic life.

Stocks and work in progress
Stocks and work in progress are valued at the lower of cost and net realisable value, after making due allowance for obsolete and slow-moving items. Costs include all direct expenditure and an appropriate proportion of fixed and variable overheads.

Research and development
Expenditure on research and development is written off in the year in which it is incurred.

2) Turnover
The turnover and profit before taxation are attributable to the one principal activity of the company all of which arises in the United Kingdom.

3) Operating profit

	2004	2003
	£'000	£'000
The operating profit is stated after charging:		
Directors' emoluments and other benefits	152	104
Depreciation – owned assets	80	70

4) Taxation

	2004	2003
	£'000	£'000
Corporation tax at 23.8% (2003: nil)	5	—

The directors consider that a provision for deferred taxation is not required as in their opinion a liability will not crystallise in the foreseeable future.

Prepayments. This term arises courtesy of the matching concept, that expenditure should be linked to the income gained as a result of that expenditure. Often expenditure is made in one accounting period, but the income is only realised (i.e. for purposes of these accounts, invoiced for) in the next one. In the first accounting period, these will have to be shown as 'prepayments'.

Accrued income is when you have done a piece of work but have not yet invoiced for it.

Accruals are the opposite of prepayments: you have made something, and part of the cost of making it comes from something for which you have not yet received an invoice.

Deferred income is the opposite of accrued income: you've sent the invoice, but haven't done the work yet.

Futura Gadgets Ltd
NOTES TO THE ACCOUNTS – continued

5) **Tangible fixed assets**	Plant & Machinery	Fixtures & Fittings	Total
	£'000	£'000	£'000
Cost			
As at 1st January	520	80	600
Additions	30	20	50
As at 31st December	550	100	650
Depreciation			
As at 1st January	230	50	280
Charge for the year	70	10	80
As at 31st December	300	60	360
Net book value			
As at 31st December 2004	250	40	290
As at 31st December 2003	290	30	320

6) **Stocks**	2004	2003
	£'000	£'000
Raw materials and consumables	50	40
Work-in-progress	30	25
Finished goods and goods for resale	65	60
	145	125

7) **Debtors**	2004	2003
	£'000	£'000
Trade debtors	190	170
Other debtors	5	—
Prepayments and accrued income	15	10
	210	180

8) **Creditors: amounts falling due within one year**	2004	2003
	£'000	£'000
Trade creditors	135	120
Other creditors	40	35
Taxation and social security	25	22
Accruals and deferred income	20	23
	220	200

Remember that the company's 'authorised' (i.e. maximum allowed) share capital is not the same as the amount of shares actually in issue.

This is just a reminder of how much has gone from the P and L account into the balance sheet.

Note that if other reserves, like a revaluation reserve, changed, this would be noted here, too.

Capital commitments. What this paragraph means is that no unusual or substantial capital commitments have been made, which do not show up in the accounts. Such commitments might include having signed an agreement to buy a property. No cash has changed hands, but the commitment is overhanging the company, and would be important to a potential investor or buyer.

Futura Gadgets Ltd
NOTES TO THE ACCOUNTS – continued

9) Share capital	2004	2003
	£'000	£'000
Authorised:		
Ordinary shares with a nominal value of £1 each	100	100
Allotted, issued and fully paid:		
Ordinary shares with a nominal value of £1 each	10	10

10) Reconciliation of movement in profit and loss account reserves	2004	2003
	£'000	£'000
As at 1st January	205	215
Retained profit/(loss) for the financial year	5	(10)
As at 31st December	210	205

11) Capital commitments

There were no capital commitments at 31st December 2004.

Appendix B: A Model Sales Pipeline

For any business that sells in decent-size chunks (i.e. large items or service contracts, as opposed to sales in a shop), sales are not binary, either 'yes, we've made a sale' or that thing that used to ring up on old-fashioned cash registers, 'no sale'. Instead, a sale is a *process*, starting with buyer interest and ending with delivery. Both the sales and finance cornerstones need to know where any individual sale is in that process. The Beermat Sales Pipeline is the tool for doing that.

First you break the process down into ten steps, then you assign a decimal to each step, as below:

0.1 The prospect is on a list

0.2 The prospect is on a properly qualified list

0.3 A 15-minute meeting with the prospect has been arranged

0.4 They appear to be a *serious* prospect: they say they have needs, and the money to pay for your solution to those needs, right now

0.5 You have some kind of proof that the above assertion is genuine

0.6 You get to do a proper, formal pitch to them

0.7 You are on a shortlist

0.8 You get a verbal yes

0.9 You get a formal yes

1.0 The money's in the bank

(Note that the steps 0.6 and 0.7 will vary from business to business. The ones shown here are typical, but not universal. What are the crucial hurdles in your sales process?)

Next, you multiply the expected value of the deal by its decimal. Then, you halve each of these sums, to be cautious, except for 0.9 and 1.0 deals. Also for caution, remove all 'deals' at 0.1, 0.2, or 0.3 stage.

Add the remaining figures up, and you have a simple revenue forecast.

For example, if you have a 15-minute meeting organised with someone who may place an order worth £100,000, have a serious prospect interested in £10,000, are pitching for another £10,000 and have a signed contract for £5,000, your Beermat Revenue Forecast is:

Phase × Amount		= Value	× Probability factor	= 'Beermat value'
0.3	£100,000	£30,000	0	0
0.4	£ 10,000	£ 4,000	0.5	£2,000
0.6	£ 10,000	£ 6,000	0.5	£3,000
0.9	£ 5,000	£ 4,500	1	£4,500
Beermat Revenue Forecast				£9,500

Of course, this is *not* a precise forecast for what you will earn in the relevant time frame: but it is as good as any other forecasting system, especially for start-ups.

When you are a bigger company and can say with some certainty, 'we usually do £200,000 in July', you can start writing £200,000 in your July cash flow forecast. But until then, we recommend that you be conservative and use this method.

The finance cornerstone should sit down *every fortnight* with the sales cornerstone and talk through the pipeline (don't just email it: meet). This is especially true in a start-up, where the selling is actually done by the sales cornerstone (as opposed to by a sales force managed by the sales cornerstone). In this case, the finance cornerstone must sales-manage the sales cornerstone. This involves asking about the progress of sales, especially those that are not making their way up the list towards 1.0, and being ruthless about taking them off the list if they remain 'stuck' for too long.

For a fuller explanation of the pipeline and its uses, read *Sales on a Beermat*.

Appendix C: A Simple Business Plan Template

What follows is not a magic formula for success, but a starting point, beyond which you must progress if you are to write a really good business plan. Templates like this should all come with a health warning: don't think that just filling in the boxes below guarantees that you have a plan that will excite readers (especially potential funders, who see loads of these). Just as you can't write Shakespeare's sonnets by dashing off 14 lines of verse with a particular rhythm and rhyming scheme, this template is the start – you have to put in your energy, excitement and belief.

Note also that you shouldn't stick slavishly to the model. There is no model that suits every business, and anyone who tells you they have a universal template is deceiving someone: possibly you, possibly themselves.

Because of the above, we nearly didn't put a template in this book at all. But we often get asked for them, so here's a Beermat Model Business Plan.

1. Caveat

If the plan is to be shown to anyone outside the company, it must, by law, come with a covering note as its front page(s), making certain legal points. These include:

★ By accepting it the reader agrees to confidentiality

★ And if they do divulge information and that damages the company, they are liable

★ It's not a perfect picture of the business, nor one that has been externally verified

★ The forecasts aren't promises

★ This 'does not form the basis of an offer for shares'

There are plenty of standard forms for these – find a way of getting a free one.

These dull things are exactly what you don't want at the start of what should be an exciting, energising document. But the law says it must go first, and there's no way round that. If it's any consolation, we have often seen investors take the caveat section, tear it off, then start reading…

2. Executive summary

This section should summarise the vision, the story and pay-off.

So:

★ Where's the pain? (In what market, and what does it consist of?)

★ What are you going to do about it? (List your main products)

★ Why will people buy from you rather than someone else (Your differentiator)

A brief paragraph on the history of the business so far, highlighting any particular successes. Please note 'brief paragraph': we've seen plans that have rambled on and on ('we moved to our new offices in 2000. Jackie Smith joined us in September of that year from Hypercorp…'). Sorry to disappoint, but the reader isn't interested! A quote from a delighted, major customer is of much more value…

> 'We are delighted with the service we have had from Hopeful Ltd, and plan to do lots more business with them.'
>
> Albert Smith, head of operations, Megacorp

A very basic outline of your plans for the future, and a justification of why you will achieve them.

Financials

★ If you are seeking funding, say how much has already been put into the business, how much you now need and why.

★ Forecast a potential value in three years' time and state the p/e ratio on which that is based.

★ Your exit strategy (if there is one).

★ Current and projected financial basics. (For example…)

	2004/05	2005/06	2006/07	2007/8
1) Turnover	273.4	1,138.2	3,478.2	7,349.4
2) Profit/(loss) before tax	(5.9)	(55.1)	240.2	771.5
3) Profit/(loss) before tax as % of turnover	–2.2%	–4.8%	6.9%	10.5%
4) Net cash in/(out) flow	20.4	21.4	12.2	284.8
5) Closing cash position	33.2	54.6	66.8	351.6

3. The commercial context

★ The basic market need you fulfil. Expand on the very brief outline of the vision in the exec summary (pain, products, differentiator).

★ The current state of your market. Size (number of potential customers, as well as a financial figure), growth rate, any other 'drivers' (main changes in legislation, technology, tastes etc.) not mentioned in previous section.

★ Enemies. Your competitors (list main ones and tell the reader something about them). Restate your differentiator. Potential substitutes, and why people won't switch to them.

★ Friends: potential strategic allies.

4. The route ahead

Remember that the plan is a map of where you are headed. What do you intend to do by when? What resources will you need to gather in order to do these things? List a few key initiatives (e.g. 'open office in Manchester') and targets (e.g. 'be the largest supplier of Xs in our region') (Note: targets also appear in marketing section).

For *initiatives*, add:

★ intended dates when you will start and when you will complete

★ any preconditions (things that need to be in place before you start)

★ any 'milestones' if it's a complex initiative

★ cornerstone responsible

★ main resources required to succeed, and their costs (years 1 – 3)

For *targets*, add:

★ intended dates when you will meet them

★ cornerstone responsible

★ main resources required to succeed, and their costs
(years 1 – 3)

Will the company keep to these schedules? Probably not. But if
they do deviate, they need to rewrite the plan.

5. People and culture

★ The top team, with brief and relevant biogs

★ Company org chart

★ Current, and future planned, headcount

★ What sort of people are you looking for?

★ How do you intend to attract them?

★ How do you intend to retain and motivate them? How will
you make it as much fun as possible?

★ Any formal incentive schemes, profit shares etc.

★ What training do you have in place/planned?

One key moment in the life of every business is when it hits that
level of around 25 people, when the culture undergoes a massive
change as it moves from 'sapling' to 'young tree'. At this point,
the team need to get together to discuss the future, to agree on
the way forward, and to take on board the fact that things are
about to change culturally. When do you anticipate this happening?

Financials

Human resource costs for current and next three years

★ Wages/salaries

★ Employer's NI

★ Budget for motivational events/'Beermat days' (etc.)

★ Training budget

6. Marketing

For each product and market:

★ How you sell – what; in what unit size; at what price; to whom; how when and where they buy

★ Objectives (we want x customers spending y per annum by 2007)

★ Any specific promotions planned?

Plus:

★ Your plans for building general awareness

Financials

Current and projected (three years') marketing spend, for each major market if appropriate. For example (we're not saying 'do all of these'!):

★ Website

★ Telemarketing (qualifying, not annoying telesales)

★ Special online campaigns (e-mailouts etc.)

★ Special customer events

★ Other promotional activities (trade shows etc.)

★ PR

★ Brochure/fliers/materials (keep to a minimum!)

★ Direct mail

7. Sales

Your sales process – what the steps are; how you move sales along the 'pipeline'; how you will be better than your rivals at each key step:

★ Your sales structure. How the team is organised. Are you centrally or locally focused (i.e. do your salespeople roam the country, or each have a regional 'patch')?

★ Your current main prospects

★ Your sales team

★ How are your salespeople motivated? (We dislike commissions, preferring a bonus based on general company performance, but we know that other salespeople disagree!)

Financials

★ Average cost of each sale (broken down by product if relevant)

★ If available, past sales figures

★ Estimated sales figures for next three years (remember, this will be a rough estimate!)

8. Operations

The story of what you do, in greater detail than in the exec summary:

★ Sourcing

★ Manufacture

★ Delivery

★ After-sales service

Financials

Breakdown of major costs in each of the above, per major product line if relevant.

9. Technology

★ Any special processes, patents etc.

★ Current R and D projects

Financials

R and D budgets (current and next three years' estimate)

Costs of seeking/maintaining patents

10. Financial forecasts and analysis

Current and projected finances in greater (but still not vast) detail. For example:

	2004/05	2005/06	2006/07	2007/8
1) Turnover	273.4	1,138.2	3,478.2	7,349.4
2) Cost of sales	(192.7)	(824.7)	(2,752.5)	(6,002.2)
3) Gross margin	80.7	313.5	725.7	1,347.2
4) *Gross margin as % of turnover*	*29.5%*	*27.5%*	*20.9%*	*18.3%*
5) Overheads	(86.6)	(368.6)	(485.5)	(575.7)
6) Profit/(loss) before tax	(5.9)	(55.1)	240.2	771.5
7) *Profit/(loss) before tax as % of turnover*	*−2.2%*	*−4.8%*	*6.9%*	*10.5%*
8) Net cash in/(out) flow	20.4	21.4	12.2	284.8
9) Closing cash position	33.2	54.6	66.8	351.6

Current and projected overheads

For example:

	2004/05	2005/06	2006/07	2007/8
1) Human resources	28.2	171.5	265.7	327.6
2) Marketing	37.2	91.1	112.3	136.3
3) Office accommodation	7.0	31.6	27.7	27.7
4) Other costs	11.6	50.4	55.8	60.1
5) Total	86.6	368.6	485.5	575.7

Funding required and exit opportunities

★ Cite amount invested so far, broken down by investor, and the resulting share structure

★ How much additional funding is needed, and what it will be spent on. (Give as detailed a breakdown as possible.)

★ If you are seeking debt funding, on what will it be secured

★ Restate the exit opportunity: what stake you are offering, and what you intend that will be worth in three years' time. What kind of exit you are seeking

Sensitivity analysis

Graphs showing what would happen to profit before tax if:

★ Sales fell

★ The price obtainable in the marketplace fell

★ Any other foreseeable and especially relevant changes in the business environment

A brief description of what measures would be taken to deal with these.

Index

The number given is for the start of the main discussion of the relevant topic

Marketing on a Beermat

Chris West

The new book from the author of the bestselling *The Beermat Entrepreneur* and *Sales on a Beermat*

The Beermat entrepreneurs are highly regarded small business advisers. In *Marketing on a Beermat*, Chris West shows you how a tight marketing budget need never be a barrier to success. Ranging from the basics of strategy and research to tips on how to generate free PR and the latest online techniques, his insights are guaranteed to give your business the edge.

The *Beermat* guides: helping you build a great business

BUSINESS
BOOKS

Sales on a Beermat

Mike Southon & Chris West
With an introduction by Stephen Fry

Bestselling authors of *The Beermat Entrepreneur* tackle sales

The Beermat entrepreneurs are highly successful small business advisers, and in *Sales on a Beermat* they demystify the most important skill that any business can possess: selling. Ranging from coverage of the basics of organising a sales team and calling on customers to insights into the psychology of successful selling, their advice will be invaluable to anyone involved in selling, particularly those running or working for small enterprises.

The *Beermat* guides: helping you build a great business

BUSINESS
BOOKS

**Order more *Beermat* guides from your
local bookshop, or have them delivered
direct to your door by Bookpost**

| **Sales on a Beermat** | Mike Southon & Chris West | 9781847940063 | £8.99 |
| **Marketing on a Beermat** | Chris West | 9781905211043 | £8.99 |

Free post and packing
Overseas customers allow £2 per paperback

Phone: 01624 677237

Post: Random House Books
c/o Bookpost, PO Box 29, Douglas, Isle of Man IM99 1BQ

Fax: 01624 670923

email: bookshop@enterprise.net

Cheques (payable to Bookpost) and credit cards accepted

Prices and availability subject to change without notice.
Allow 28 days for delivery.
When placing your order, please state if you do not wish to receive
any additional information.

www.rbooks.co.uk

BUSINESS
BOOKS